H-ρ

Why People
DON'T
Believe

WHY PEOPLE
DON'T
BELIEVE

Confronting
Seven Challenges
to Christian Faith

Paul Chamberlain

BakerBooks
a division of Baker Publishing Group
Grand Rapids, Michigan

Published by Baker Books
a division of Baker Publishing Group
P.O. Box 6287, Grand Rapids, MI 49516-6287
www.bakerbooks.com

Printed in the United States of America

Library of Congress Cataloging-in-Publication Data
Chamberlain, Paul, 1954–
    Why people don't believe : confronting seven challenges to Christian faith / Paul Chamberlain.
        p.   cm.
    Includes bibliographical references (p.   ) and index.
    ISBN 978-0-8010-1377-5 (pbk.)
    1. Apologetics. 2. Christianity and atheism. I. Title.
BT1212.C43 2011
239—dc22   2010044371

11 12 13 14 15 16 17   7 6 5 4 3 2 1

To James, whose wit and ability to see the humor in everyday events have provided steady respite from the serious contents of this book. Writing it was easier because of you.

Contents

Acknowledgments

As every author knows, books do not come into existence without the aid of others. This book was given early impetus by Howard Anderson, the dean of the Association of Canadian Theological Schools, a division of Trinity Western University, where I teach. I will never forget one particular discussion with him where I shared my concern regarding the specific challenges to religion and the Christian faith that eventually became the topic of this book. His encouragement to analyze the challenges and write this book was the motivation I needed to get started, and the sabbatical I was granted for this purpose was critical to the successful completion of the project.

Along the way I was blessed with feedback from many throughout North America who listened to me lecture on these challenges and provided vitally important feedback. Some were supportive, while others threw their own challenges my way. I grew in my understanding through both and will be forever grateful for audience members who interact in these ways.

David Lunn and Tyler Chamberlain deserve special mention for their research assistance and the series of interrogations they subjected me to on both the content and style of the text as it was being written. Not only is the book decidedly different because of their input, but it is safe to say that, thanks to them, I have already been forced to defend most of the ideas I present as mine in the book.

My greatest appreciation, however, goes to my family: Gail, Tyler, Raechel, and James. Their support and encouragement have never wavered in spite of many late dinners and professionally induced absences as I worked on this book. They provide a constant center and foundation in the midst of a fast-paced world.

1

The Power of Religion

The young man makes his way through the crowds. Under his jacket is strapped a bomb. The city park is filled to capacity. It is a national holiday, so people from across the region have taken time out to come and celebrate. Everyone is in a festive mood as they eagerly look forward to the concert and fireworks to follow. Young children hold balloons and streamers, and the aroma of barbeques grilling steaks and burgers fills the air.

The young man is alone and unnoticed by anyone else as he takes a seat near the platform where the band will soon play. A few feet in front of him is a young couple obviously deeply in love. The young woman is talking animatedly to her partner about the new engagement ring she is planning on showing her parents this evening when they arrive at the park. The young man watches as a growing number of people move toward him to get seats close to the band.

An emcee walks onto the platform and welcomes the people. The area around the young man is now full. He reaches under his jacket and pulls a pin, setting off a bomb destroying himself and all those within twenty feet of him. Chaos and screaming erupt as human debris flies in all directions. The plan has worked perfectly.

The young man's friends soon learn of his actions and, while they grieve over the loss of their dear friend, they know he is now in heaven. What is more, he has dealt a horrific blow to the infidels, and that is a cause for celebration.

This story is fictional, yet as anyone living in the twenty-first century knows with grim clarity, it is alarmingly realistic. Nothing about it is an exaggeration of events that have occurred hundreds of times in the past few years alone. The young man, while fictional, represents hundreds of real people, also usually young, who are ready and willing to carry out actions like those of this young man.

With a similar story, Sam Harris, American neuropsychiatrist and outspoken atheist, opens his book *The End of Faith: Religion, Terror, and the Future of Reason*, which launches a full-frontal assault on religion and the destruction it causes in our world. We know very little about the young people who carry out such horrific actions. Why then, asks Harris, is it so easy for us to guess their religion?[1]

Harris began writing his book on September 12, 2001, the day following the infamous terrorist attacks of 9/11. He was deeply provoked by these events, and his reasoning in the book is straightforward, if perhaps oversimplified: if young men were slaughtering people because they believed their religion commanded or encouraged them to do so, then perhaps religion, with its outdated and pernicious superstitions, should be eradicated to make the world safe for the human race.

To many of us, *The End of Faith* may sound like a lament, but for Harris and others, it represents a great step forward for humanity. He is simply one author among a growing chorus of voices expressing a deep fear of religion and faith in our world—a fear that, at times, is blended with hostility and suspicion.

He pursues his fictional story further and inquires what we can infer about the young man from his actions. Was he popular in school? Was he rich or poor? Was he of high or low intelligence? Did he have a college education? Was his future bright or rather bleak? Harris concludes that the young man's actions provide no answers to any of these questions or hundreds of others like them. There simply is very little we know about him. Then comes his final question: "Why is it so easy, then, so trivially easy—you-could-almost-bet-your-life-on-it easy—to guess the young man's religion?"[2]

What is it about religion that stirs such intense passion? Simply put, religion is perceived as having a power unmatched in our world to move people to commit atrocities, to carry out actions that violate every dictate of conscience and human decency. To borrow Harris's own words, religion has become "a living spring of violence" in our world.[3] Some of our most cherished beliefs, he says, are leading us inexorably to kill one another, and the fact that a generation of poor and illiterate children are being fed into fundamentalist religious schools around the world should terrify us.[4]

The situation is more serious than most people seem to think, Harris contends. Our very survival as a human race may be at stake, he warns, and he is not alone in voicing this concern.[5] Thanks to advances in technology in the past fifty years, especially in the art of war, our religious "neighbors" are now armed with chemical, biological, and nuclear weapons. As far as Harris and others like him are concerned, anyone who is not afraid of the potential harm this represents simply has not given the matter due attention. Words like *God* and *Allah* must go the way of *Apollo* and *Baal* lest they destroy us all.

Our situation is this, explains Harris: most people in the world believe the Creator of the universe has written a book. We have the misfortune of having many such books in existence, each making a claim of exclusive infallibility. People tend to organize themselves into factions according to which of these incompatible claims they accept. This means that while a spirit of ecumenism and liberalism has touched every religion here and there, the central tenet of every religious tradition is that all other religions are in error in their most basic teachings or, at the very least, dangerously incomplete. For this reason, to quote Harris, "Intolerance is thus intrinsic to every creed."[6]

It is not just acts of *religious violence*[7] that are part of the negative impression of religion in the public consciousness. The charges against religion go beyond these horrific actions, but as we will see later in this book, many of the other charges are connected in some way with violence.

My experience of lecturing and interacting with groups throughout North America on this issue has led me to conclude that most Christians are simply unaware of the litany of allegations being brought against religion, including Christianity, by its new twenty-first-century critics. The usual knee-jerk response by Christians when they hear such allegations is to airily dismiss them with retorts such as, "This is just more of the same old thing we have come to expect." Or they may smile and say, "Those people must not know much about faith and religion. How can they make such statements about us and our faith?" The problem is that neither of these replies takes the allegations seriously or even attempts to understand them. Interestingly, when these allegations are laid out in greater detail and Christians begin to catch a glimpse of the message and passion of the critics, they are usually shocked and bewildered.

The allegations call into suspicion the nature of God, the morality of God, certain religious doctrines, and more. As mentioned earlier, British evolutionist and atheist Richard Dawkins describes God as "arguably the most unpleasant character in all fiction: jealous and proud of it; a petty, unjust, unforgiving control-freak; a vindictive, bloodthirsty ethnic cleanser; a misogynistic, homophobic, racist, infanticidal, genocidal, filicidal, pestilential, megalomaniacal, sado-masochistic, capriciously malevolent bully."[8] More will be said later about this description of God.

Furthermore, these allegations against religion were given a focal point on one horrifying day: September 11, 2001. We all remember it. In fact, most of us know where we were upon first hearing the news. It was a day that changed the world in a number of significant ways, one of which concerns the way people think about religion. Suddenly religion became important, showing up on the radar screen like never before. We were pushed, some of us kicking and screaming, into the realization that a personal, private religion is not what many religious people have in mind. Far from it. No matter how strongly we in the West wished to go about life minding our own business and hoped others would do the same, we were hit with the realization that this was a pipe dream, unrealistic in the extreme. Things were suddenly different; the religio-cultural transition took one day.

Unfortunately, it didn't stop with 9/11. Since that infamous day, there have been many similar events on a smaller scale, and the cumulative effect has been immense. The striking result is that many of our friends and neighbors have become increasingly open to the claim advanced by Harris and his colleagues that religion is a dangerous force for evil and unless it is eradicated from the world, our survival as a human race may be in jeopardy. A new fear and suspicion of faith is beginning to take hold, not just in the ivory towers of academia or journalism but in the broader culture, and we for whom faith is important dare not ignore it. This growing skepticism toward religious faith of all stripes extends throughout the Western world.

Newsweek magazine recently reported the growing trend toward religious opposition in an article entitled "The New Naysayers."[9] It sampled Harris's writings as well as those of British biologist Richard Dawkins and American philosopher Daniel C. Dennett, author of *Breaking the Spell*. In this book Dennett marvels at the controlling power religion has to hold people captive. He writes, "We often find human beings setting aside their personal interests, their health, their chances to have children, and devoting their entire lives to furthering the interests of an *idea* that has been lodged in their brains. . . . How did just one species, *Homo sapiens*, come to have these extraordinary perspectives on their own lives?"[10]

The *Newsweek* article also reminisces about the not-too-distant challenges to religion in the writings of Friedrich Nietzsche as well as the landmark lawsuit filed by Madalyn Murray O'Hair in 1963. Numerous other leading news magazines have also reported on this phenomenon, and the same critics of religion are normally highlighted in these articles.

What does all of this mean for people of religious faith? What does it mean for Christians attempting to live out and contend for their faith? At the very least it means that while many of us seem to take it for granted that our faith is a force for good in the world and is viewed as such by most others around us, the reality of how religion is perceived is far different. Religious belief is no longer seen by many of our friends and neighbors as a means to resolve humanity's deepest problems. Instead it is increasingly regarded as *being* the problem, the villain, the culprit of our times. Indeed, many view it as the cause of some of our greatest evils: violence, intolerance, imperialism, irrationality, bigotry, and war, to name a few. Can there be greater evils than these in our world? It is not hard to see why someone who believes religion has fostered and encouraged such evils would also believe we would be better off without it.

As I considered this challenge to faith, two areas of need became evident. The first is the need for people of faith to hear and truly understand the concerns and challenges raised against religion. We simply must get to the bottom of what it is about religion and faith that stirs such resistance and passion in some people. I have often reminded my students that we are not in a position to respond to objections raised against our faith until we understand them and are able to express them in a way that is recognizable by those who voice them. Doing this will require that we keep our cultural ears open, listening to a variety of media voices that have the attention of North Americans such as popular movies, musical artists, heavily used websites, and widely read magazines.

Second, there is a need to engage in thoughtful and frank dialogue with those who raise such objections. Part of living out one's faith includes the constant readiness to give an answer to people who wonder how one can justify the teachings of that faith. This is especially true in the current environment in which most of our fellow citizens are all too familiar with the evil and havoc wreaked on the world in the name of religion. People deserve an answer, and as the New Testament itself states unequivocally, we are called to give them one (1 Peter 3:15 and Jude 3).

For these reasons, I have three aims in this book. First, I hope to accurately represent the concerns and challenges raised against religious faith, particularly those raised against Christianity. I will avoid all sugarcoating of the objections, and to accomplish this I will draw directly from the writings, lectures, or interviews by the critics themselves.

My second aim will be to respond to these challenges, and it is important to say something about how I plan to do so. I write as a Christian: a person who is committed to the belief in the existence of the biblical God, to Jesus of Nazareth as the revelation of God in human form, and to the truth of the Christian Scriptures as interpreted by the major creeds of the Christian church. I make no claim to represent all religious traditions, nor do I think anyone could do so fairly or accurately. Having said that, it is worth noting that the new critics of religion routinely contend the problem is not with any one religion, whether Christianity, Islam, Hinduism, or any other. Rather, it is with religion per se. In fact, when they point out faults of specific religions, they almost always do so in order to demonstrate this very point—that the problem lies not with any one religion but with religion as a phenomenon. Consequently, some of my responses will necessarily include replies to charges involving other religions. On the whole, however, I prefer to leave the task of representing those other faith traditions to those within them.

My responses to the challenges will center around two foundational questions: First, are the new critics of religion right to identify *religion* as the cause of the world's greatest evils, or have they missed something in their analysis and taken aim at the wrong target? I believe the latter and will devote part of this book to demonstrating this.

Second, is *Christian* faith guilty of the evils the critics accuse religion of? I am not asking whether *individual* Christians have carried out wrongful actions. That is hardly a question worth considering. Rather, is Christian faith, when correctly understood, guilty of the charges the new critics are bringing against religion, or have the critics misunderstood something about the Christian faith? Again, I believe the latter, and this will be another focus of this book. Part of my response will relate directly to the Christian faith.

My third aim is the most positive one. Once we have replied to the charges of violence and evil, we will be in a position to take the discussion to the next level and examine the many good and humane contributions Christianity has made to the world throughout the past two thousand years. My contention here will be that not only is Christianity, properly understood, free of the main allegations leveled against religion by the twenty-first-century critics, but it is the source of great good in the world. In fact, the impact of Christianity for good upon human civilization is nothing short of breathtaking. Unless you have previously inquired into this subject, I predict you will be surprised and deeply encouraged by what you read in the chapter devoted to this issue. Many of the good things in our world that we in the West simply take for granted and could hardly imagine the world without exist as a direct result of the impact of Christianity upon the world. I have come to see this as an integral part of replying to the charge that Christianity is a dangerous force for evil and we would be better off without it.

This book is intended to operate as a public response to the challenges to religious faith mentioned in chapter 2. I trust it will also act as a guide for concerned Christians seeking to learn how best to interact with their friends, neighbors, and colleagues who harbor deep suspicions toward their faith. My hope is not only that those who make the case against religion are given the chance to rethink their position, but also that Christians who read these pages will see how they can engage others around them who launch these charges against their faith.

I must admit I also harbor the hope that this book, and other similar works by Christian authors, will invite responses from members of other traditions to join the conversation by writing comparable books from their own traditions so we can have constructive dialogue. Certainly, if there ever was a time when such dialogue was needed, not only among people of religious faith but also between religious and nonreligious people, it is now in the current religious-cultural environment.

In the next chapter I will set out the case against religion and faith as it is currently being made by some of religion's most vocal critics in the twenty-first century: Sam Harris, Richard Dawkins, Daniel Dennett, Christopher Hitchens, and others. If you are a person like me whose faith is important to you, you will no doubt find the contents of this chapter unsettling. The case against religion *is* unsettling. Having read a good bit of the literature, I believe it is meant to be so. The authors are deadly serious about the critical nature of our current situation and are pulling no punches when leveling their attacks on religious belief and practice. Indeed, for them this is a matter of life or death, survival or destruction. It is not a time for niceties or delicacy.

Perhaps a caveat is in order here. I have been speaking of the *new* critics of religion and of a *new* set of charges being brought against religion. Lest I give the wrong impression, let me say at the outset that, of course, hostility toward religion or people of faith is not a new or specifically twenty-first-century phenomenon. Indeed, it was back in 1963 that Madalyn Murray O'Hair, possibly America's best-known anti-religion activist, won her landmark lawsuit against mandatory classroom prayers in America. She later founded the group now known as American Atheists. When a chaplain, visiting her in the hospital, once asked how he could help her, she is reported to have famously replied, "Drop dead." Going back further still, Sigmund Freud, Karl Marx, and many of their followers showed an antipathy toward religious faith, and Jesus was crucified by an angry mob for his teachings. Clearly, anti-religious hostility is nothing new.

What is new in the current atmosphere then? Simply put, 9/11 brought with it a new fervency, even militancy, in the approach taken by the critics of religion who are actively dedicated to getting out the message that religious faith is not only false but actually dangerous to humanity and we would all be better off without it. Indeed, as far as many of the critics are concerned, eliminating religion may be the key to the very survival of the human species. That momentous day pushed us into a new era, and we can never return to the way things were. We can only find a way forward.

2

Reason to Fear

I have never witnessed a time of greater fear, suspicion, and even hostility toward religious belief. This fear of faith is permeating the current atmosphere of our Western culture. Anyone who pays the least bit of attention to news stories, scans recent *New York Times* bestseller lists, or listens to the occasional talk show will be well aware of this growing fear. As noted in the previous chapter, this hostility has been stimulated by a number of widely reported acts of violence and terrorism that were motivated by religion. Who among us has not heard of the 9/11 terrorist attacks, suicide bombings around the world, acts of violence done against abortion clinics, or even Andrea Yates, the distraught mother who drowned her five children to protect them from Satan? How could anything that motivates such acts of destruction be good? When we think of it, can we really blame people for being suspicious of religion when acts like this are done in the name of God?

A number of critics of religion have been rightly disturbed by events such as these and have capitalized on them to develop a passionate case against religion, complete with arguments and supporting data. This case has been carried to a very concerned public throughout Western culture by means of bestselling books and a host of other media, and it has molded people's thinking about religion and faith. The striking result is that religion is now viewed more negatively than at any other period in recent history. It is time for us to put this case against religion on the table so we can analyze it to see what force it has.

Religion Breeds Violence

The first and foundational charge against religious faith in the twenty-first century is that religion breeds violence and shocking abuses of human dignity. In other words, in spite of all the talk about loving others and promoting peace and goodwill, religion has actually produced the opposites of these, and in deadly doses. This theme is common to all the new critics of religion, and it represents the most important message they wish to communicate to the public.

Their reasoning is straightforward: suicide bombings, violent actions against abortion clinics, and the like are ultimately explainable by people's beliefs. Beliefs are not merely academic or theoretical entities. They are the things that define our vision of the world, and if religion is about anything, it is about beliefs. Many of our beliefs are harmless, but some are not because there is a clearly established link between belief and action. Some of our beliefs are inherently dangerous, say the critics, and examples are not hard to find.

One sobering instance, according to Sam Harris, is the belief held by some that they are members of a chosen people living in a corrupt culture that is seducing their young people away from the faith, and that they will be rewarded in heaven beyond their imagination for killing members of that culture. When people believe this, he asserts, it is a simple task to find some of them who are willing to fly planes into buildings.[1]

The point is that a few of our most cherished beliefs are leading us to kill one another. Which ones? Very often our religious beliefs, and the reason for this is not hard to see, say the critics. The most fundamental belief of every religion, almost without exception, is that God wrote a book, their book, the one they base their religious teachings on. The absolute and unquestioned truth of such books is a foundational part of what religious people believe, and terms like "infallible" and "without error" are common descriptors of such books.

Our situation is this, says Harris: There are many different religions, so there are also many different holy books—all, of course, written by God. These books differ on many things, hence the distinctive teachings of the various religions. But Harris notes that they have a perverse agreement on one thing of fundamental importance: they all teach that the other holy books are filled with falsehoods or, at best, are dangerously incomplete. Thus intolerance is intrinsic to every creed. An attitude of respect for other holy books or for the views of other religious adherents is neither encouraged nor accepted. As history has repeatedly shown, this intolerance leads to conflict between believers of different faiths and also between believers and unbelievers. Opponents are labeled as *infidels*, *apostates*, *enemies of God*, and the like, and all too often this conflict ends in violence and horrific abuse of other human beings.

As Harris is fond of saying, the content of holy books is accepted with unquestioned assent. No evidence for their claims is needed since the content emanates directly from God; no higher authority could ever challenge its truth. Thus it is immune from critique or the type of assessment we normally apply to our sources of information.

Sometimes critics of the faith are frustrated by what they see as unwillingness on the part of many Westerners to face the harsh reality that religion is the cause of violence. The very idea is a bitter pill to swallow for many who were raised thinking of their holy book as *the good book* and who were brought up believing that religious activities such as attending church and praying lead to good character and action, not evil. Many would rather find the causes of such violence anywhere but in religion, and they point to all sorts of factors such as poverty, inequality, lack of opportunity, or frustration on the part of this or that group of people—anything but religion—as the real causes. The new critics will have none of this face-saving exercise for religion.

To make his case that the problem really is with religion and not something else, Harris calls upon his readers to simply ask *why* Muslim terrorists do what they do, or *why* abortion clinic bombers do what they do. Why, he asks, would Osama bin Laden, who was neither poor, uneducated, or a victim of American aggression, devote himself to killing thousands of men, women, and children he had never met? Why would a young parent, sibling, aunt or uncle, grandchild, niece or nephew who had never been personally wronged by an abortion provider put him- or herself at great personal risk of jail or even execution by blowing up an abortion clinic and killing those inside? Or again, why did nineteen well-educated, middle-class men give up their lives and future hopes for the privilege of killing thousands of civilians they had never met?

The answer to these questions is obvious, says Harris, if we will just face the facts. Bin Laden, the 9/11 terrorists, and the abortion clinic bombers really believe what they say they believe. The nineteen young men who boarded those flights on 9/11 believed they would be rewarded by going straight to paradise. It is rare to find human behavior so fully and satisfactorily explained, he adds. Subtract the Islamic belief in martyrdom and jihad and the actions of suicide bombers and the jubilation that invariably follows their deaths becomes unintelligible. Insert these beliefs, however, and one can only marvel that suicide bombing is not more widespread.[2] Beliefs are the fundamental causes of our actions, and unfortunately, religious beliefs in particular are leading to many acts of violence.

The problem of religious violence is nothing new, say the new critics of religion, even though it has sprung into public focus in a fresh way in recent years. The entire Inquisition, beginning in 1184 and running for hundreds of years, was an exercise in using torture of the most unimaginable kinds to root out heresy and enforce orthodoxy. Torture was the preferred method of persuading confessing heretics to name those with whom they had collaborated in sin and also of forcing witnesses to testify against others.

And who, asks Harris, were these torturers and informers—the commanders of these actions? They were men of God, popes, bishops, friars, and priests—people who had devoted their lives to the service of Christ.[3] And note their reasoning behind this practice: if torture was an appropriate treatment for those who broke the laws of men, how much more fitting it must be for those who broke the laws of God. Richard Dawkins suggests that United States founding father John Adams may have been thinking, in part, of the Inquisition when he declared that the Jewish and Christian revelation had become "the most bloody religion that ever existed."[4]

The Inquisition may be over, but widespread violence in the name of religion is not. Most of us know full well, says Harris, that virtually all the recent conflicts on the world stage are motivated by tensions between religious groups. In Palestine, Jews and Muslims fight each other, while in the Balkans, Orthodox Serbians and Catholic Croatians try to destroy each other. In Northern Ireland, Protestants and Catholics are at war with one another, while in Kashmir it is Muslims versus Hindus. In Sudan it is Muslims versus Christians versus animists, while in Nigeria, Muslims and Christians are at odds. Throw weapons of mass destruction into the mix and you have a recipe for

Armageddon. British journalist and author Christopher Hitchens has perhaps gone the furthest, bluntly stating his own view that "the main source of hatred in the world is religion."[5]

Furthermore, it is not any one specific religion that is viewed as the problem; rather it is religion per se. Speaking to appreciative students at the University of Toronto in 2006, Hitchens declared, "Look anywhere you like, to slavery, to the subjugation of women as chattel, to the burning and flogging of homosexuals, to ethnic cleansing, to anti-Semitism, for all of this, look no further than a famous book that is on every pulpit in this city, and in every synagogue and every mosque."[6]

For this widely read journalist and others like him, religion is not simply *amoral* but *immoral* since it is putting our very survival as a human race at risk.[7]

But aren't we really talking about religious extremists here? This is an objection often raised in response to Harris and others. Don't we all realize that it is only those on the radical fringes of the various religious traditions who are perpetrating acts of violence in the name of their religion? Don't we recognize that they make up only a small percentage of the adherents in any religious tradition? Surely we admit that the vast majority of religious believers are moderates who live out their faith far differently from the radical extremists and thus are exempt from the charges leveled against them.

Many who proudly identify themselves as religious moderates may be surprised to learn that the new critics of religion heap scorn on what we call religious moderation, regarding it as possibly worse than religious extremism. How can they view it in such poor light? In the first place, they view religious moderation as nothing more than a failed attempt at religious accommodation of culture and intellectual knowledge gained since the various ancient religious texts were written. In the view of the new critics of religion, moderates are only relaxing their standards of adherence to ancient superstitions while otherwise maintaining a belief system that was passed down to them from people who were, relatively speaking, ignorant of the world.

Second, the critics say religious moderation lacks integrity by being unfaithful to the religious texts, which themselves are unequivocal in their teaching. If one is not going to be faithful to one's own religious Scriptures, then why hang on to the religion at all? In other words, religious moderates have already rejected some of the teachings found in their religious texts because they regard them as incompatible with knowledge gained in the past few hundred years. Having done so, ask the critics, wouldn't it be more honest simply to abandon the religion altogether as an unreliable guide to knowledge and truth? Religious moderates wish to have it both ways, and the critics view that as a lack of integrity.

The critics say, however, that the worst problem with religious moderation is that it provides the context in which extremism can grow and in which religious violence can never be fervently opposed. Without mainstream religion, or religious moderation, religious extremism would not have found the home it has, and thus it would lack the respectability, power, and resources it currently possesses to carry out acts of violence.[8] For these reasons, religious moderation, far from being superior to religious extremism, is really the villain behind it. Without it, religion simply would not breed the violence it does.

This raises the question: If religion leads to violence and abuse as the critics say, why does it do so? Is there some feature or characteristic built into the fabric of religion that causes it to be a destructive force? Not surprisingly, the critics believe there is such a feature, and the one they point to will come as a surprise to many people of faith. Religion is irrational from the bottom up, say the critics, and this deep irrationality is ultimately behind much of the violence caused by religion. Consequently, it represents one of religion's most scandalous failings, and the critics are scathing in their attacks on it. It is to this charge against religion that we now turn.

Religion Is Irrational and Lacks Evidence for Its Claims

The alleged irrationality of religion is viewed not merely as one defect among others; it is seen as a foundational flaw in religion because it prepares the ground for many others and, in fact, gives rise to them. Without this problematic feature, many of the other evils the critics point to in religion would not arise.

The charge is this: religion gets people to believe stunningly irrational things for which there is no evidence. Because religion has this uncanny ability, when it comes to our religious beliefs, we lack the constraints that normally guide us in decisions of whether to accept or reject claims we encounter. Richard Dawkins contends that in most of life's day-to-day issues and decisions we all, including religious

people, usually know the difference between what is rational or reasonable and what is not. When we come across an irrational idea,
we either reject it outright or enjoy it as good fiction, but we don't
believe it to be true. Yet religious people, he says, seem to drop all
such distinctions when it comes to their religious beliefs. Something
about religion gets them to believe ideas that are just as irrational as
fairy tales, myths, or make-believe.

Sam Harris agrees and illustrates the point in a recent interview
with *Newsweek* magazine where he notes a confusing inconsistency
among Christians. On one hand, most of them would require as much
evidence as anyone else upon hearing that their spouse is cheating or
that yogurt can make a man invisible. On the other hand, however,
they are willing to accept claims about an invisible divine being, a
divine book, and the need to believe every incredible idea in that book
for fear of divine sanction, with no evidence whatsoever.[9]

The accusation is that in religion there seems to be literally no
limits to what people are willing to believe, and the fact that there is
a lack of evidence for these beliefs presents no obstacle whatsoever
to believers. Calling this "a special problem for religion,"[10] Harris
asks with bewilderment how it is that in this one area of life we have
convinced ourselves that "our beliefs about the world can float entirely
free of reason or evidence."[11] This charge against religion is virtually
taken as a given by critics such as Harris, Dawkins, and Hitchens.
It is a theme found either explicitly or implicitly throughout their
writings on religion.

We may wonder what is so wrong with people believing things others think are weird or unjustified. Aren't people free to believe whatever
they like? Is this charge against religion really as serious as all this?

Yes it is, say the critics, and its seriousness stems from the fact
that the beliefs we are speaking of—religious beliefs—are not merely
academic or theoretical. Far from it. The things religious people believe make a real difference in the lives of others and in the world
in which we live. Religious beliefs are not merely irrational, say the
critics, but in their irrationality they are leading their adherents to
carry out the kinds of actions mentioned earlier: suicide bombings,
abortion clinic attacks, and the like—acts that are violent and immoral by any reasonable standard of justice. In Harris's words, "As
a man believes, so he will act." Dawkins agrees and quotes Voltaire
approvingly: "Those who can make you believe absurdities can make
you commit atrocities."[12]

Furthermore, because religious beliefs "float entirely free of reason and evidence,"[13] they are untestable. There is no way to determine their truth or to adjudicate between them when such evidence-free propositions conflict with one another as they surely do among the religions of the world. None can be shown to be superior or inferior, closer to the truth or further from it, or more or less worthy of our belief.

Further still, those who hold such religious beliefs are immunized from being persuaded or even influenced by others. We may discuss our day-to-day beliefs and convictions regarding politics, philosophy, gardening, and so on with those around us. After hearing new perspectives or arguments, we may adjust, add, or even drop a belief. It is the normal intellectual journey we are all on. When it comes to religious beliefs, however, the critics say things are different. These beliefs, unlike all others, are impervious to debate and discussion. After all, where does one begin if one wants to critique a person's religious beliefs or encourage him or her to reconsider them if that person holds these beliefs not because evidence has led him or her to them but rather because they were received from a divine being? This kind of belief paves the way for suicide missions, abortion clinic bombings, and so on, and the world finds itself helplessly watching as the violence unfolds. Once a person's beliefs are cut free of evidence, there is nothing we can do to change or influence them.

Where does religion get this astonishing power to cause people to believe ideas, even irrational ones, without evidence and act on them in such atrocious ways? How does it have such unimaginable control over people? This question is especially perplexing when we realize that we are talking about people whose actions in the rest of life are normal and rational; they are ordinary, thoughtful people except when it comes to their religious life.

Dawkins has a ready explanation, and it is neither profound nor mysterious. Religion, he asserts, exercises a very simple technique. It glorifies unquestioned obedience; it does so from the cradle to the grave, and the effects are unspeakable. Speaking recently of religiously motivated terrorists he says,

> However misguided we may think them, they are motivated . . . by what they perceive to be righteousness, faithfully pursuing what their religion tells them. They are not psychotic; they are religious idealists who, by their own lights, are rational. They perceive their acts to be good, not because of some warped personal idiosyncrasy, and not because they

have been possessed by Satan, but because they have been brought up, from the cradle, to have total and unquestioned *faith*.[14]

Could anything be simpler? Religious leaders, says Dawkins, have discovered that if from early on they drive home to believers the concept that the teachings of their religion originate in a divine being, those teachings will be regarded as beyond question. It is a brilliant technique that puts astonishing power over the minds of believers into the hands of religious leaders. We neither debate nor evaluate messages that come to us from the mouth of God; the only proper response is to believe and accept them. Once the unquestionable authority of religious statements is accepted by the faithful, the rest follows naturally and the stage is set for horrific acts that the world is powerless to stop.

The critics see this technique in all religions, not simply Western ones. Richard Dawkins approvingly quotes Nehru, a founding father of postcolonial India and an atheist, who declared that the religion he saw in India almost always stood for "blind belief and reaction, dogma and bigotry, [and] superstition."[15] In other words, this is a technique of religion per se rather than of any particular religion. It's just the way religion works.

Furthermore, the irrationality of religion is not limited to peripheral ideas of religious life and teaching—ideas one could take or leave as a believer. It runs through the very heart of religion, extending to many core beliefs such as the Christian doctrine of a trinitarian God. What on earth could it possibly mean, Dawkins asks incredulously, to say that Jesus is *consubstantial*—of the same substance or essence with God? What substance? What essence? He derisively quotes the *Catholic Encyclopedia*, which cites the words of the historic Athanasian Creed to define the doctrine of the Holy Trinity: "The Father is God, the Son is God, and the Holy Spirit is God, and yet there are not three Gods but one God."[16] As far as Dawkins is concerned, the irrationality is obvious.

What about the very existence of a divine being in the first place? Nothing could be more foundational to virtually every religion than belief in a God or gods, and yet Harris wonders how anyone could hold such a belief. Rhetorically he asks how our understanding of the universe is advanced by believing in a Creator who communicates through a one-way process of revelation. Thinking specifically about the Christian God, he also wonders how people can believe in a supposedly benevolent and all-powerful God who would permit events like tsunamis that destroy thousands of people in a few horrific hours. If God is benevolent and omnipotent, surely he would both *desire* and *be able* to give better treatment than this to people he supposedly created and loves.[17]

Dawkins launches into the question of the actual scientific evidence for God's existence and boldly contends that evidence is sparse in the extreme. It is not that the idea of God is unprovable, he declares. Belief in the existence of God should be seen as a scientific hypothesis like any other, and as such, it must be discoverable in principle if not in practice. If God exists and chose to reveal himself to us, he could clinch the argument once and for all. But no such evidence exists, at least none that is persuasive in the least, says Dawkins.

He critiques St. Thomas Aquinas's five ways of proving God's existence and, not surprisingly, finds them all wanting. This was probably unwise on his part because as Alister McGrath notes, "He is clearly out of his depth, and achieves little by his brief and superficial engagement with these great perennial debates."[18] We will comment further on his critique of Aquinas's five ways later in this book.

Not only does Dawkins find evidence for God's existence exceedingly weak, but he is mystified by the attitude he sees in some Christian thinkers toward the notion of evidence. In this vein, he raises an idea put forward recently by Oxford theologian Richard Swinburne, who wondered aloud whether God has purposely given us only so much evidence.[19] Dawkins is flabbergasted by this notion and believes it betrays a deep hostility toward evidence on the part of religious believers. In the end, all he can say is that if this is the best the theologians can do (and Swinburne is emeritus holder of one of Britain's most prestigious professorships of theology), then perhaps we do not want a theologian. This point warrants further analysis, and we will return to it later.

Dawkins also comments on what he views as a favorite trick employed by religious people trying to prove the existence of God, namely their tactic of shifting the burden of proof to atheists and calling upon them to prove there is no God. Dawkins will have no part of this tactic and responds by drawing upon the story of the Celestial Teapot told by prominent mathematician and atheist Bertrand Russell in his 1952 book *Is There a God?* He contends that this fictional creature and a few others such as the Tooth Fairy, Mother Goose, and the Flying Spaghetti Monster of cyberspace make it clear that the burden of proof rests with believers, not unbelievers. What matters, he argues, is not whether atheists can disprove God. They cannot, he concedes rather easily, any more than any of us can disprove the Tooth Fairy or the orbiting Celestial Teapot. What matters, he believes, is not whether God's nonexistence can be proven but whether God's existence is *probable*, and it most assuredly is not.[20]

We will examine the question of burden of proof later in this book when we also analyze a number of other aspects of the charge of irrationality brought by the critics of religion. But it is important to note one other foundational facet of this charge. The critics argue that not only is religion irrational in general but, more specifically, it is also inherently anti-scientific and thus has stood as an enemy of the discovery of knowledge and the progress that has come with it for centuries. It is to this allegation that we now turn.

Religion Is Anti-Scientific

If we think our knowledge of the world and universe is impressive now, imagine where it would be if it weren't for the continual obstacles religion has put in the path of such understanding. The ways of religion are intrinsically opposed to the ways of science, say the critics. This is important because science is viewed as a firm and reliable way of acquiring knowledge of our world. Thus religion is seen as the constant enemy of such knowledge, discovery, and the progress that comes with it. Any progress in human knowledge will have to come from the world of science, whose members will be locked in an eternal battle against religion, which stands ready to suppress any new discovery. In his book *The God Delusion*, Dawkins writes that people who hold their Scriptures in high regard, or *fundamentalists* as he labels them,

> know they are right because they have read the truth in a holy book and they know, in advance, that nothing will budge them from their belief. . . . The book is true, and if the evidence seems to contradict it, it is the evidence that must be thrown out, not the book.

Conversely, Dawkins states:

> I, as a scientist, believe . . . not because of reading a holy book but because I have studied the evidence. It really is a very different mat-

ter. . . . As a scientist, I am hostile to fundamentalist religion because it actively debauches the scientific enterprise. It teaches us not to change our minds, and not to want to know exciting things that are available to be known.[21]

In the same vein, Sam Harris describes science as the discipline that "represents our most committed effort to verify that our statements about the world are true (or at least not false)." We do this "by observation and experiment within the context of a theory."[22] On the other hand, he says, religious people believe what they do because God wrote it in a book, their particular Scriptures. This puts religious beliefs "beyond the scope of rational discourse." They "float entirely free of reason and evidence." And when it comes to the question of verifying our beliefs, he adds that "most religions offer no valid mechanism by which their core beliefs can be tested and revised." After all, why would a person want to test and revise beliefs that come from God? This leads him to define religious faith as "simply unjustified belief in matters of ultimate concern . . . belief, in the absence of evidence."[23]

The idea here is that while science is in the business of developing wonderful methods for exploring and understanding our universe, religion stands as a persistent enemy of the entire scientific enterprise. In other words, if we take our religious faith seriously and believe in the authority of our Scriptures, we will be at odds with science. This means that in order for science to make any headway at all it must continually resist the forces of religion or they will suppress the scientific enterprise altogether.

Later in this book we will devote careful attention to this charge concerning the anti-scientific nature of Christianity. In the meantime, in the light of this charge, it is interesting to note Dawkins's own puzzlement as a scientist by what he calls some "genuine specimens of good scientists" who are sincerely religious. He refers specifically to Arthur Peacocke, Russell Stannard, Rev. John Polkinghorne, and Francis Collins. "I remain baffled," he says, "by their belief in the details of the Christian religion: resurrection, forgiveness of sins and all."[24] How, he wonders, can people who are used to judging their every assertion by the rigorous demands of evidence suddenly believe such things for which there obviously is no evidence? He throws up his hands and has no answer except to assert that they simply cannot mean what they say.

The overall charge that religion is inherently irrational along with the subsequent allegation that this irrationality leads religious believers to carry out atrocious acts of violence represents a serious critique of religion. At this point members of my own faith tradition, Christianity, will no doubt object strenuously to the way this portrayal of religion reflects upon their own faith. Their objection will run along the following lines: this may be the way things are for religion in general, but not for Christianity. Leaving aside other faiths for the moment, Christianity has a deeply embedded preventive measure, namely the Bible's own teaching on such actions, which is designed to prevent Christians from carrying out the kinds of horrific acts mentioned earlier. In other words, biblical moral teaching makes it clear that God does not call a person to carry out violent and atrocious actions; in fact he condemns such actions. So if Christians are guilty of committing such acts not, it is the fault not of the Christian faith or the Bible but of the individual. Aren't these Christians themselves to blame for failing to understand the full and complete teachings of their own faith, in short for failing to read their own Bibles?

It's a good question, and the answer, say the new critics of religion, is a resounding no. Biblical morality is not the panacea many in the Western world seem to view it as. It is, in fact, appalling if one looks at it honestly. So taken are these critics with the abysmal nature of biblical moral teaching that it forms the basis of one of their main charges against Christianity, which is not an insignificant charge. Whereas most Christians tend to view Christianity as a wonderfully positive exception to the causes of violence in our world, the critics paint it in just the opposite way: as a religion whose very moral teaching sanctions bloodshed and violence. It is to this charge that we now turn.

Biblical Morality Is Appalling and Promotes Violence

I am often invited to give guest lectures at universities and other public venues on topics relating to faith and religion. When I do, I nearly always make a point somewhere in my talk of encouraging my listeners to read the Bible for themselves and do their own thinking about what it says and means rather than let others interpret it for them. Over the years I have found this to be a strategic piece of advice that has appealed to people who regard themselves as independent thinkers, the way most of us do.

On one occasion, however, I gave my customary you-should-read-the-Bible-for-yourselves talk while participating in a debate format in one of Canada's major universities; but this time the response from my debating opponent, a local professor of philosophy, was different. He quickly proclaimed that he had done exactly that as a young man when he was thinking of becoming a theologian and pastor like his grandfather. He emphasized that he had read the Bible—all of it—with great care and then added with a certain glee that his reading of the Bible was precisely the reason he was *not* a Christian. By reading it for himself, he had learned what the Bible really taught, especially on matters of morality, and he proceeded to list a veritable catalog of atrocious actions performed by God's people in the Old Testament, some of which were commanded by God. Following that he set out a series of appalling commands, allegedly given by God for his people to live by. He concluded his summary of the matter by proclaiming that the God of the Bible is worse than Hitler, worse even than Satan, and that anyone who was willing to honestly face up to his acts and commands as recorded in the Bible would see this. In responding this way, this professor gave voice to an allegation against Christianity that has grown in prominence in recent years.

Many Christians are simply shocked to hear this charge brought against their faith. And no wonder; it is a striking charge. The new critics of religion in the twenty-first century have seized upon this charge with great passion, but there is a difference now. They have added a new element to this old charge against *Christianity* that links it together with their overall case against *religion*, and in the process they argue that this problem in biblical morality is, if anything, even more important now than ever. We'll explore this link shortly. For now though, what is the basic charge against biblical morality?

It is this: biblical moral teaching and action is simply immoral. Contrary to what most people believe about the noble nature of biblical moral teaching, the critics claim it violates any decent standard of justice and morality. They argue that if we read the whole Bible honestly, we will be unable to ignore this harsh reality about biblical morality unless we are willing to throw out everything we know about good and evil. This is said to be especially true of the Old Testament, but the New Testament does not entirely escape the charge, as we will see shortly.

But there is more, say the critics. It is not just the moral *teaching* of the Bible that is immoral, as if it were some isolated entity unconnected to anything; obviously the *God behind the moral teaching* is immoral as well. He must be; after all, he is the source of the teaching. If it is immoral, then it follows that he is too. If anyone denies this, argue the critics, they should just look at the Bible to see what God did there, and instances of his immoral actions will not be hard to find. The God of the Bible violates his own commands, most notably the command against killing. He is also harsh and vindictive, going way overboard in handing out penalties and judgments.

The story of Noah is one of Dawkins's favorites. While Christians around the world teach this story to their children as an example of great faith and obedience on Noah's part and great power, justice, and compassion on God's part in acting mightily to judge sinners and save those few who were faithful to him, Dawkins sees the moral of this story as downright appalling. It is not that he believes this story actually happened; he is quite sure it did not. What alarms him is the frighteningly large number of people who do believe it is historical—approximately 50 percent of the United States electorate plus millions of others around the world—and the effect it has on those believers.

According to Dawkins, it is belief in stories like Noah's flood that caused Asian holy men to blame the 2004 tsunami not on a plate tectonic shift, as any scientifically informed person living in the twenty-first century should have, but rather on human sins ranging from drinking and dancing in bars to breaking certain Sabbath rules. This kind of belief, declares Dawkins, also caused American televangelist Pat Robertson to reportedly blame the 2005 catastrophic flooding in New Orleans on a lesbian comedian who lived in the city. The practice of blaming people for natural catastrophes is pernicious, he says, and is a direct result of the influence of religion.[25]

God's excessive harshness doesn't end with the flood; far from it. In fact, Dawkins wonders whether those people who hold up the Bible as an inspiration to moral rectitude have the slightest notion of what is actually written in it. Do we know, he wonders, that in the Old Testament book of Numbers God commands Moses to attack the Midianites because they stand in the way of his people gaining access to the Promised Land, and when the soldiers carry out the command but spare the women and children, Moses was infuriated?[26]

Do we also know, he pointedly asks, how misogynistic the God of the Bible is? He calls his readers to consider the story of Jephthah, the military leader, and compare it to the equally bizarre story of God commanding Abraham to sacrifice his son Isaac on the mountain. In the latter case, at least God stops Abraham the split second before his knife plunges into Isaac, and the boy is spared. Things are different in the case of Jephthah, however, who bargains with God that if he helps the army win a particular battle, he will sacrifice the first thing to walk out of his door upon his return home. To his sorrow, his daughter comes rushing out of the house to greet her father, and Jephthah has no recourse, so he kills her, or as Dawkins puts it, he "cooked her."[27] In this case, Dawkins acidly points out, God did not see fit to intervene as he had in the case of Isaac. The misogyny is clear. We will return to these biblical incidents and respond to Dawkins's charges concerning them later in this book.

Things get worse. Dawkins is outraged by the offenses for which God issued the death penalty in the Old Testament book of Leviticus: cursing one's parents, adultery, making love to your stepmother or daughter-in-law, homosexuality, marrying a woman and her daughter, and bestiality. In the case of bestiality, Dawkins caustically notes, the unfortunate beast is to be killed too. Sam Harris also examines capital offenses in the Bible and wonders why anyone would "take moral instruction from a book that calls for stoning your children to death for disrespect, or for heresy, or for violating the Sabbath."[28]

Again, what shocks Dawkins is not that such stories and accounts are true. They probably aren't, he says repeatedly. The shocking part is that people in the twenty-first century are willing to base their lives on such an appalling role model as the God of the Bible whom, as we have already seen, he summarily describes as "arguably the most unpleasant character in all fiction: jealous and proud of it; a petty, unjust, unforgiving control-freak; a vindictive, bloodthirsty ethnic cleanser; a misogynistic, homophobic, racist, infanticidal, genocidal, filicidal, pestilential, megalomaniacal, sadomasochistic, capriciously malevolent bully."[29] Fortunately, he says, it's a good thing that few of us, including religious people, derive our morality from the Bible.

But doesn't the Bible contain many good commands, actions, and principles—principles that any of us would be wise to live by? Yes it does, Dawkins agrees, and he proceeds to list a few: the instruction to pay our taxes; the command to abstain from cheating, killing others, and engaging in incestuous relationships; and the call to not do anything we would not wish to be done to us. He adds, however, that these good principles are buried alongside others that no decent person would wish to follow, and the Bible supplies no rules or criteria for distinguishing the good principles from the bad. The upshot is that even the value of the good commands is deeply diminished.

Why then is the charge of *biblical immorality* so important to the critics as they make their case concerning the *evils of religion*? What is the link, the connection between the two? The link, says Dawkins, consists in the fact that the immoral biblical teaching one finds in the Bible paves the way for same kind of immoral, violent, vicious, homophobic, or otherwise atrocious actions carried out by some religious people today. Such actions have been the subject of great media attention in recent years, and they are also the focus of the new critics' case against religion. The point is that biblical moral teaching makes these kinds of actions easier to carry out and may even provide a kind of justification for them—or at least so say the critics.[30] This link is allegedly what makes this biblical teaching so destructive and pernicious.

Lest anyone make the mistake of thinking this link is purely theoretical and not really very important, Dawkins refers to a study carried out by Israeli psychologist George Tamarin that, he argues, highlights the disastrous effects of this atrocious biblical morality on people's attitudes and actions today.[31] In the study, Tamarin presented the account of the battle of Jericho in the Old Testament book of Joshua to more than a thousand Israeli children ages eight through fourteen.

> Joshua said to the people, "Shout for the Lord has given you the city. And the city and all that is within it shall be devoted to the Lord for destruction. . . ." Then they utterly destroyed all in the city, both men and women, young and old, oxen, sheep, and asses, with the edge of the sword. . . . And they burned the city with fire and all within it; only the silver and gold, and the vessels of bronze and of iron, they put into the treasury of the house of the Lord.

Tamarin then asked the children a straightforward question about morality: "Do you think Joshua and the Israelites acted rightly or not?" They were given three choices: total approval, partial approval, or total disapproval. Sixty-six percent gave total approval, 26 percent gave total disapproval, leaving 8 percent in the middle with partial approval. When asked to comment on why they answered the way they did, the children said things like the following: "In my opinion Joshua was right when he did it . . . [because] God commanded him to exterminate the people so . . . Israel will not . . . assimilate amongst them and learn their bad ways," and "Joshua did good because the people who inhabited the land were of a different religion, and when Joshua killed them he wiped their religion from the earth."

Before moving to part two of Tamarin's experiment, it is worth noting a comment Dawkins inserts about these rationales offered by the children. Palestinian children, he says, who are brought up in the same war-torn part of the world would very likely offer equivalent opinions in the opposite direction, showing the immense power of religion, especially when inculcated from an early age, to divide people and foster historic enmities and vendettas. It is these kinds of considerations that fill Dawkins with despair.

But Tamarin's experiment was not over. For part two he gathered a different group of 168 Israeli children and gave them the same text from Joshua, but this time Joshua's name was replaced by "General Lin" and "Israel" was replaced by "a Chinese kingdom 3,000 years ago." When the question was asked this way, the experiment gave opposite results with only 7 percent giving total approval of General Lin's behavior and 75 percent disapproving.

What Tamarin showed, says Dawkins, is that when religious loyalties were removed, the majority of the children agreed with the moral judgments that most modern humans would make, namely that Joshua's action was barbaric genocide. And the real clincher, to use Dawkins's words, is that it was religion that made the difference between children *condemning* genocide and *condoning* it.

These are tough accusations and difficult Old Testament stories that even many Christians find puzzling. But others will vigorously protest at this point that Dawkins is being unfair and selective in his treatment of the issue because he is leaving out the most important moral teacher of all in the Bible, and that is Jesus of Nazareth. What about his moral teaching and that of the New Testament in general? Don't things look entirely different there? In fact, isn't Jesus one of the world's greatest moral teachers, and isn't this agreed to by virtually everyone?

Dawkins's answer may surprise some. Yes, he concedes, Jesus was a great improvement over the "cruel ogre of the Old Testament."[32] In fact, he calls Jesus's teaching in the Sermon on the Mount a set of moral instructions that were way ahead of their time. Jesus, he says, actually anticipated Gandhi and Martin Luther King Jr. by two thousand years when he called his followers to *turn the other cheek* (Matt. 5:39). Dawkins even reminds his readers that he once wrote an article entitled "Atheists for Jesus" and was later delighted to be presented with a T-shirt bearing that legend.

There is a catch, however—an exceedingly big catch. True enough, Jesus's moral teaching is superior to that of the Old Testament, but

Dawkins contends that this very moral superiority bears out his point because the places where Jesus's teaching is superior to Old Testament moral teaching are precisely the places where he departed from the Old Testament and did not derive his moral teaching from it. As an example, Dawkins points to Jesus's challenge to the religious leaders' dire warnings about keeping Sabbath laws. Their laws were harsh and unreasonable, so Jesus departed from them. Decent people do not derive their moral teaching from the Scripture, Dawkins says repeatedly, and neither did Jesus. That is why it was better than Old Testament morality.

Dawkins's moral evaluation of the rest of the New Testament is not much better than of the Old Testament. In the New Testament, he and other recent critics of religion charge, there are doctrinal teachings that are scandalous and dangerous and that contribute to the immoral and violent character of religion. A number of these doctrines come under withering attack from the new critics, and these attacks constitute another of the main charges leveled at Christianity by its new critics. It is to this charge that we now turn.

Religious Teaching of an Afterlife Is Scandalous and Dangerous

A short time ago I attended a funeral for a young man, age seventeen, who had been struck by an oncoming vehicle that had crossed into his lane, killing him instantly. He had just driven his mother to work and was running an errand before heading to school in the morning. The young man was a star baseball player and was also popular and well loved, which was obvious from the rows of young people and teachers in the audience. It was one of the saddest funerals I have attended. Friends surrounded the grieving parents and offered comfort, but what is that compared to the loss of your son?

There was, however, something that offered them profound comfort. They held the firm belief that their son, a follower of Jesus, was now with Christ and that, while they missed him deeply, they would see him again one day. In fact, as the officiating minister put it, the young man was more certain than any of us that when a person places faith in Christ, absence from one's physical body means being present with Christ.

It is hard to imagine anything that could be more comforting for parents walking such a difficult road, especially when we compare it with the lack of hope offered by the opposite belief that our deceased loved ones are gone forever, period. On one side is profound hope and comfort; on the other, sheer hopelessness and emptiness.

Imagine how distressing it would be for parents such as these to be informed and eventually to believe that this comforting teaching is not only a pipe dream but actually a scandalous and dangerous teaching that gives rise to great evils in our world and we would be wise to rid ourselves of it. How can it be that the same teaching that provides such comfort and encouragement to some people elicits such vigorous condemnation from others? Where is the alleged danger, the scandal?

Even the critics of religion recognize the comforting power of this doctrine, but their evaluation of its ultimate impact on our world is radically different from that of most religious believers. Sam Harris explains it this way: We all know or learn very quickly that life on this planet is a mix of good and bad, with the ratio depending upon factors that are usually beyond our control. Such factors include the time and place of our birth, the circumstances into which we were born, our ongoing health, our appearance, and so on. Philosophers call these *accidents of birth*; some of us are simply luckier than others. Even for the so-called lucky ones, however, life on this planet leaves much to be desired. We are all painfully aware that at any time we could lose our health, wealth, spouse, children, parents, and everything else that is dear to us. We may be terrified at losing any of these, but the reality is that we *will* lose them all one day. It is not a possibility; it is a certainty, and we all know it.[33]

Harris ruminates on this gloomy state of affairs and comments on the high level of stress and despair it causes for most of us, even those who have it pretty good in this world. He is right. The undeniable fact is that most people in the Western world spend great amounts of time and money trying to distract themselves from this morbid fact. But their efforts are largely unsuccessful. Widespread human despair is a common subject of books, articles, and lectures throughout the world, and the natural question that arises is whether there is any way out of the despair. Is there a solution to this depressing state of affairs?

Yes, answers Harris. Religion has come to our rescue, or so it claims. It has invented a cure for all of this, namely the doctrine of the afterlife. What an idea! Can anyone think of a better way out of the disappointment that is life on this earth than this doctrine? We may lose the things we love in this life, but we can get everything we want *after* we die. Few ideas could have greater appeal to human beings caught in the predicament of life on this planet or greater power for providing comfort and encouragement in the face of overwhelming odds. It is no wonder someone came up with this idea, and religion is perfectly positioned to be its source.

For all its blissful comfort, however, there is another deeply ominous side to the belief in an afterlife, says Harris. Hope and comfort are not all this belief produces. The harsh reality, he contends, is that it would be hard to find a teaching that has been the source of more evil and destruction in our world than the idea that an afterlife awaits us if we simply do the will of God. Indeed, it is not an exaggeration to say this religious belief could threaten the very survival of the human race. These are strong words, and Harris means them sincerely. Pressing his point, he asks a question we raised earlier, namely, why did nineteen well-educated, middle-class men give up their lives and future hopes for the privilege of killing thousands of civilians they had never met? The answer is agonizingly obvious: they believed they would go straight to paradise for doing so. The men who committed the atrocities of 9/11 were not cowards or lunatics in any ordinary sense of those terms. As it turns out, they were men who believed in an afterlife. They were men of faith, and Harris declares that we should finally acknowledge that this is a terrible thing to be.

We must never forget, he points out, drawing from the words of the Qur'an, that many people around the world believe that the men who brought down the World Trade Center towers are now seated at the right hand of God amid "rivers of purest water, and rivers of milk forever fresh; rivers of wine delectable to those who drink it, and rivers of clearest honey" (Qur'an 47:16). These men who slit the throats of stewardesses and delivered young couples with their children to their deaths at five hundred miles per hour are at present "arrayed in garments of fine green silk, and rich brocade, and adorned with bracelets of silver" (Qur'an 47:20–21).

Indeed, the appeal of paradise is so powerful and the consequent willingness to be martyred so robust that one failed Palestinian suicide bomber, on whom Harris reports, described himself as being "pushed" to attack Israelis by "the love of martyrdom. . . . I didn't want revenge for anything. I just wanted to be a martyr," he testified.[34] As Harris acerbically puts it, "A single proposition—*you will not die*—once believed, determines a response to life that would otherwise be unthinkable."[35]

Michel Onfray, author of the book *In Defense of Atheism*, poignantly summarizes the deleterious effects on the thinking of those who believe in an afterlife. Singling out Christian faith specifically, he argues that the Christian doctrine that there is something beyond science and beyond our senses "devalues the only life we have and makes us too prone to violence."[36] This is, to say the least, a new and startling twist on a well-known and loved teaching of Christian faith.

Could the doctrine of an afterlife actually threaten human survival? As outrageous as this suggestion may sound, consider the following scenario described by Harris as he struggles to get the attention of a sleeping Western world that refuses to label the terrorist threat for what it is—a religious threat. An Islamist regime acquires long-range nuclear weaponry. Such a regime, Harris notes, will not be deterred from using such weapons by the threat of death or of mutual destruction. Notions of martyrdom, fueled by belief in the afterlife, will see to that. If history teaches us anything, we will probably not know precisely where the offending warheads are or what their state of readiness is, so we will not be able to rely on conventional weapons to destroy them. What are our choices in such a situation? Our only option for survival, Harris suggests, may be a nuclear first strike of our own. This would be unthinkable—killing tens of thousands of innocent people—yet what other option would there be?

Such a scenario is insane, concedes Harris, and yet, he also insists, it is a plausible one by which much of the world's population could be annihilated because of religious ideas, especially belief in the afterlife. This is a teaching, he says, that should be viewed in the same way as we view Batman, the philosopher's stone, and unicorns.[37] The doctrine of the afterlife is not only mythical, it is possibly the most dangerous myth to crop up in a long time.

Certain religious *beliefs*, including this one, are scandalous, say the critics, but they are only part of the problem. Something else about religion aggravates the situation, and that is the kind of *attitudes* it engenders in its adherents. Our underlying attitudes always influence the way we express and live out our beliefs, and the same is true of religious people. What are these offending attitudes that are encouraged by religion?

Religion Engenders Intolerance and Exclusivity

It is safe to say that in recent decades the notions of *tolerance* and *inclusivity* have risen virtually to the level of supreme cultural values in the Western world. We appeal to them on every imaginable question, whether to stake out the moral high ground for ourselves by showing how tolerant and inclusive we are or to show the error of anyone who disagrees with us. "She is intolerant!" we cry, and who needs to say more? If this accusation sticks, our unfortunate victim is seen to have violated one of society's cardinal virtues and is now on the defensive. She is someone we can safely ignore, maybe even marginalize. Religion is charged with violating these two cardinal sins, and it is a serious charge indeed.

Before examining how this charge goes, let us ask why tolerance and inclusivity have become so important in Western culture. It was not always this way. Alan Bloom's analysis in his well-known book *The Closing of the American Mind* provides helpful insight on this question. Writing in the 1980s, he points out that belief in absolute truth has come to be regarded by many people in the West as the prime cause of some of the world's greatest problems, including racism, bigotry, war, imperialism, marginalization of minorities, and so on. A person who believes truth is absolute will tend to say things like, "I'm right and you're wrong," rather than simply, "We disagree, so let's just leave it at that and not worry about who is right." In other words, the idea that one's own views are correct and those of others are false is undergirded by the belief in absolute truth. And of course, once people believe their point of view or way of life is right, it is not a great step to grant themselves permission to impose it on others who hold false views or live wrongly. Who knows, we might even be doing them a favor.

It is not surprising then that inclusivity and tolerance have come to be regarded as our greatest cultural virtues, says Bloom. And the way to be tolerant and inclusive is clear; it is to reject the notion of absolute truth. By eliminating it, we undercut the basis for intolerance and exclusivity and we are free to be tolerant of all viewpoints.[38]

Bloom's analysis is, if anything, more telling today than when he wrote it since most Western countries have continued to become even more diverse and pluralistic. The people around us represent a great variety of cultures, religions, and moral views, and tolerance and inclusivity are seen as essential attitudes if we are to make this vastly diverse situation work. They are the keys to getting along with each other with all our differences. It is no wonder intolerance and exclusivity are viewed with such contempt by many around us.[39]

How then does religion, allegedly, violate these near-sacred virtues? It does so, say the new critics of religion, by making truth claims that are held to be true not only for the believers but for everyone. And here we come to a fatal flaw in the very makeup of religion, at least as far as the new critics are concerned. This flaw consists in the teaching of any given religion (alongside everything else they teach) that believers possess absolute truth about certain very important matters that other people do not have. Religious teachings are held to be universally true, even if millions of people do not presently recognize their truth, and this leads to a deep intolerance of other viewpoints and belief systems. As Sam Harris puts it, "The central tenet of every religious tradition is that all others are mere repositories of error or, at best, dangerously incomplete. Intolerance is thus intrinsic to every creed."[40]

In other words, to be religious is ultimately to be intolerant and exclusive. The stinging implication of this assertion is that religion is a major cause of division among members of the human community who already have enough trouble figuring out how to get along with each other. It creates the conviction within religious people that they and their group have the truth on important matters and others do not. Richard Dawkins labels this phenomenon a commitment to absolutism and speaks of its evil effects this way: "Absolutism is far from dead. . . . Such absolutism nearly always results from strong religious faith, and it constitutes a major reason for suggesting that religion can be a force for evil in the world."[41]

Why is this a so-called fatal flaw? Indeed, why is it considered a flaw at all to teach that one's religious beliefs are true? Very simply, because it is a very small step from *believing one is right* on such important matters as life, death, eternal destiny, and the rest to *being willing to impose* these ideas onto people who do not share them. Are we not, in fact, doing them a favor by imposing the truth on them, even if they do not see it that way? And, say the critics, religious believers have been all too willing to take this step and impose their ideas, sometimes violently, onto an uninviting world. This leads to the final charge against religion that we will consider.

Religion Leads Believers to Impose Religious Teachings on Others

Here is where it all comes together. The primary current complaint against religion, as we have seen, is that it moves believers to carry out acts of violence. But *how* does religion induce otherwise decent people to do deeds this atrocious? The answer to this question is simple, say the new critics. It is found in the very insistence on the absolute truth of religious teachings that we noted in the previous section. Once religious teachings are regarded as absolutely true and good for all people—even those who do not recognize them as such—it is a small step to being willing to impose these teachings onto others, and sometimes violent means are employed.

There are many ways of imposing one's religious beliefs onto an unwelcoming world, but the ultimate and most menacing way is through acts of violence. Through such acts we strike fear into the hearts of those on the outside. We get their attention. We let them know we mean business and are willing to go to any length necessary to see our religious truths and values spread around the globe as our religion calls us to do. After all, it is all for the good of those being imposed upon regardless of whether they recognize it.

Richard Dawkins is quick to draw the connection between *religious absolutism* and the *willingness to impose* religious beliefs onto others, and he finds many examples. In his view, the attitude toward homosexuality held by certain Christians in the United States, whom he refers to as the "American Taliban," epitomizes this phenomenon. Not only do these Christians condemn homosexuality as immoral, but many are also actively working for legislation to make it illegal, with some dreaming of the day when Christians take over and eliminate all rights of homosexuals.[42]

Dawkins sees similar attitudes toward abortion, stem cell research, and euthanasia, and he is scathing in his attack of people who are doing everything they can to stop these practices, even, he says caustically, "to the point of preventing medical research that would certainly save many lives."[43] The worst examples of imposing absolutist values on an unwilling society, however, are violent acts such as the shootings of doctors who provide abortions in North America or the suicide bombings around the world.

To show that this is not merely alarmist rhetoric, Dawkins quotes such people as Gary Potter, president of Catholics for Christian Political Action, and Randall Terry, founder of Operation Rescue—both American organizations. Potter has allegedly promised that "when the Christian majority takes over this country, there will be no satanic churches, no more free distribution of pornography, no more talk of rights for homosexuals . . . pluralism will be seen as immoral and evil."[44] Terry offered this warning to physicians who provide abortions: "When I, or people like me, are running the country, you'd better flee, because we will find you, we will try you, and we'll execute you."[45]

Dawkins emphasizes that people who utter statements like these and who carry out religiously motivated acts of violence are not necessarily psychopaths. They see themselves as good, moral people, guided by God, and that is the point we must grasp if we want to understand religion's role in the violence. They are dangerous, he says, but not dangerous psychopaths. Rather they are *dangerously religious*. Religion is the problem, and it should be rooted out if we want to undercut the basis for people imposing their values onto others. Indeed, if we do not deal with this problem, we are in danger of losing, at the very least, our liberties and, at worst, human civilization itself.

In his book *Letter to a Christian Nation*, Sam Harris speaks of the seriousness and urgency of this situation for the very survival of civilization. Referring to certain Christians who, due to their belief in a coming Armageddon that will usher in a new world, actually look forward to nuclear war as a way of speeding up the second coming of Jesus, he calls on his readers to consider the implications if a significant number of US government officials really believed the world would end soon and that this would be a glorious event. Since half of all Americans appear to believe this on the basis of their religious teaching, this should be viewed as an emergency by us all, Harris argues.[46]

To state the obvious, serious challenges have been leveled against religious faith by intelligent people who mean business. What does this mean for people of faith? At the very least it means religious belief is no longer seen by many of our fellow citizens as a means to resolve humanity's deepest problems, if it ever was. Rather, many view religion itself as the problem to be dealt with, that it is the cause of some of the world's greatest evils including violence, irrationality, intolerance, imperialism, and war, to name a few.

What should people of faith do in the light of these harsh attitudes toward religion and faith? Is there a way forward apart from abandoning faith altogether? Astronomer Carolyn Porco offers the intriguing suggestion that science itself should attempt to supplant God in Western culture by providing the benefits people find in religion—things like community and a sense of awe. "Imagine," she writes on the science website Edge.org, "congregations raising their voices in tribute to gravity, the force that binds us all to the Earth, and the Earth to the Sun, and the Sun to the Milky Way."

Porco finds spiritual fulfillment in exploring the cosmos, and some will certainly find her suggestions appealing. But I, for one, cannot help wondering how many people would be satisfied by this type of religio-scientific experience. She admits that for "people who want to know that they're going to live forever and meet Mom and Dad in heaven, we can't offer that."[47] Exactly, and this brings up what is perhaps the biggest problem with suggestions like this, namely, that they ignore the reality that we humans are incurably religious or spiritual. With almost no exceptions, wherever humans are in the world, we find religious life. This fact about humans is why academic disciplines such as the philosophy of religion exist, where scholars try to understand and assess this worldwide phenomenon. But if religion is not going away, then what is the way forward?

3

Religion and Violence

A Closer Look

Are things really as bad for religion as the new critics say they are? Does religion truly breed violence, or might the real cause lie elsewhere? This is a large question, and it is time for us to ask it. Doing so will involve thoughtful analysis of the case against religion. It will also require that we take note of a number of other facts relevant to this question and explore how they apply to it. In short, it is time for us to evaluate these serious allegations against religion.

The Reaction of Religious People to Religious Violence

As I initially reflected on the critics' allegation that religion causes violence, the first thing that caught my attention was the way religious people, almost without exception, react to acts of violence done in the name of religion. Most people of faith I know or hear about are as shocked and outraged by them as anyone else in society, and in some cases far more so. Many, in fact, are personally offended at the thought of being lumped into the same group as those carrying out such vicious acts. Perhaps I should be surprised by this, but I am not. The fact is that the religious people I come across, with few exceptions, are decent, kind, law-abiding, and generous with their time and money, so their reaction to acts of violence is no surprise.

This is true not only of people in my own faith tradition, Christianity, but of religious people in general. A friend of mine was living in Pakistan on 9/11 and vividly recalls his experience on a train there a few days after that terrible day. The train was filled with devout, religious Muslims, and the topic of discussion was 9/11. Given the media reports one often reads, some might wonder what kind of sentiments would be expressed toward the attacks of 9/11 by these religious people. On the train that day there was unanimous and passionate denunciation of the attacks by everyone. My friend listened as the devout Muslims he spoke with condemned the attacks as horrific and wrong.

So what is going on here? How can the Dawkinses, Harrises, and Hitchenses of the world point the finger at religion as the cause of the violence and cruelty while at the same time the vast majority of religious people are outraged by these very acts of violence? Something has gone wrong, but what?

Confusion of Extremism with the Mainstream

As I read and listened more to the new critics of religion, I began to notice a disturbing trend that may, at least in part, explain this conundrum. That trend is the failure on the part of some of them to distinguish between *extremists* within various religious groups and the *mainstream* adherents to those groups. This distinction is vital for anyone who desires to understand the teachings of a particular religion or worldview, as a few of my own experiences have made evident.

Over the years I have participated in a number of public forums and media events on prominent social and worldview questions where a variety of perspectives were represented. These have involved issues such as the existence of God, moral foundations, and a variety of specific ethical dilemmas. At a number of these events, I have encountered people who can only be described as embarrassing supporters. Sometimes they ask questions at public lectures or call in to radio talk shows and make statements I could never endorse, yet at the same time they publicly identify themselves with my position and claim to speak in support of me. The same people sometimes write letters to the editors of their local newspapers or even organize pickets at public events to proclaim their message. Every group has them, whether Christians, Muslims, atheists, Darwinians, Marxists, or others. British philosopher Alister McGrath refers to them as extremists and weirdos in the ranks, and in the worst cases, he says, they constitute a "lunatic fringe" within their various groups.[1]

Such people are usually an embarrassment to most others in the group for whom they supposedly speak. They do not represent the views of the vast majority of its members, yet they feel free to speak publicly on their behalf. To make matters worse, these embarrassing supporters are often given more attention and air time than their numbers warrant due both to their zealous desire to fight their battles in public and to the seeming need of the media to publish radical minority views as a way to increase ratings. Whatever the reasons, the result of the increased air time is that extremists within the group often appear to the outside world as official spokespersons when they are no such thing.

What this means is that whenever we take it upon ourselves to describe and assess the teachings of a group other than our own, we must do so with great care lest we attach undue weight to the voices of extremists within that group. If we fail here, we run the risk of portraying a minority, extreme view that is rejected by most members of the group as if it were the belief system of the mainstream. To paint all members of any group with the same broad brush, in other words to ignore this distinction between *mainstream* and *extremists*, is to misrepresent the views and beliefs of the vast majority of the people one is supposedly talking about. It is flawed reasoning and leaves one open to the charge of committing the *straw man fallacy* whereby we argue against a false distortion of a position rather than the actual position and then claim we have discredited it. Could it be that some of the new critics of religion are committing this fallacy in their assessment and denunciation of religion?

Consider some of the people Richard Dawkins quotes as representatives of Christianity. One is Gary Potter, president of Catholics for Political Action, whose warning we referred to earlier. He declared, "When the Christian majority takes over this country, there will be no more satanic churches, no more free distribution of pornography, no more talk of rights for homosexuals. . . . Pluralism will be seen as immoral and evil and the state will not permit anybody the right to practice evil."[2]

Another is Randall Terry, founder of Operation Rescue, also mentioned earlier, who proclaimed in reference to abortion providers that "when I, or people like me, are running the country, you'd better flee, because we will find you, we will try you, and we'll execute you. I mean every word of it. I will make it part of my mission to see to it that they are tried and executed."[3]

Statements like these make many in the general public fearful of the prospect of religious people gaining political power, and Dawkins is outraged by them. What he does not seem to realize is that so are most Christians, and often more than he because it is they who feel the sting of having their views misrepresented in public. I have never met even one Christian, Catholic or Protestant, who endorses the plans of action laid out by Potter or Terry in those statements, although I have no doubt that there are a small number who would.

Still another representative is the late Reverend Jerry Falwell, who made a well-known statement calling AIDS not just God's punishment of homosexuals but his punishment for a society that tolerates them, namely the United States. Huge numbers of Christians, including many who had an enduring respect for Falwell, neither agreed with this particular statement nor held any such views about AIDS. In fact, according to some reports, Falwell himself thought better of the comment and later retracted it. In any case, the viewpoint he expressed in no way represents the views of the majority of the Christian community, a fact left unmentioned by Dawkins.

Dawkins goes so far in his misrepresentation of Christianity as to include the widely discredited Pastor Fred Phelps of the Westboro Baptist Church as though he somehow speaks for the Christian church. Dawkins correctly describes him as a preacher with an obsessive dislike of homosexuals and goes on to describe at some length his antihomosexual website and his hateful activities across North America, which include picketing the funeral of Coretta Scott King where he and his followers held signs proclaiming: "God Hates Fags and Fag-Enablers! Ergo, God hates Coretta Scott King and is now tormenting her with fire and brimstone."[4]

While Dawkins includes Phelps as a representative of Christianity, the vast majority of Christians regard him as a deep embarrassment to their faith, with some I have spoken to going so far as to wonder if he is a genuine Christian at all. The nearly unanimous reaction of Christians throughout North America to him and his followers is one of head-shaking amazement and disgust, usually followed by asking, "Who are these people?"

Alister McGrath is particularly appalled by Dawkins's misrepresentations and points out another flaw such misrepresentations indicate in a person's reasoning. It is worth quoting him directly on this point.

> There is, I suppose, a lunatic fringe to every movement. . . . One of the most characteristic features of Dawkins's antireligious polemic is to present the pathological as if it were normal, the fringe as if it were the center, crackpots as if they were mainstream. It generally works well for his intended audience, who can be assumed to know little about religion and probably care for it even less. But it's not acceptable. And it's certainly not scientific. . . . Dawkins simply treats evidence as something to shoehorn into his preconceived theoretical framework. Religion is persistently and consistently portrayed in the worst possible way, mimicking the worst features of religious fundamentalism's portrayal of atheism.[5]

McGrath's hard-hitting contention in these statements is that by presenting fringe extremists as though they are the mainstream, Dawkins is drawing his conclusions about religion first and then forcing the evidence to fit these conclusions. This is an odd procedure to see coming from a noted scientist.

But there is a deeper problem still with Dawkins's misrepresentation of religion, one that points to a fundamental weakness in his case against religion. McGrath pinpoints this weakness in the following words: "Dawkins clearly has little interest in engaging religious believers, who will simply find themselves appalled by the flagrant misrepresentation of their beliefs and lifestyles. Is the case for atheism really so weak that it has to be bolstered by such half-baked nonsense?"[6]

It is a good question and a highly significant one for Dawkins's allegations against religion. His portrayal of religion, in this case Christianity, is so inaccurate that most Christians would simply not recognize their own faith in his descriptions of it. If one needs to resort to such distortions and straw men to make one's case for anything, it is usually a sign of a weak case. On the other hand, if there is no need for this kind of misrepresentation, then why do it? Let us put this more directly. If in order to argue his case that religion breeds violence Dawkins finds it necessary to misrepresent religion by ignoring the distinction between *mainstream* adherents and *extremists*, then why should we think religion breeds violence at all? Why not think it is extremists within religious groups who breed it—the very types

Dawkins himself refers to—especially since the mainstream adherents are appalled and outraged by the violence? But religious extremists do not represent their groups; they are usually an embarrassment to them.

And this raises yet another very practical problem for Dawkins's program. It means that any legitimate criticisms of religion he may bring forward will tend to be lost as suspicion grows that he has no intention of seriously critiquing religion at all, at least not as it is held by the vast majority of religious believers. He is satisfied to ridicule a distortion of it.

Clearly the distinction between extremism and the mainstream is indispensable for any legitimate analysis of a group, and especially so when the group one examines is not one's own. The fact that this distinction is ignored by some of the new critics of religion may begin to explain the huge dissonance between the charge that religion promotes violence and the reaction of outrage by religious people to these very acts of religious violence.

But perhaps we need to go further and ask different questions than we normally ask about this topic. Many discussions about the connection between religion and violence tend to focus on the question of whether religion has had a role in bringing about violent acts. That is an easy question to answer. Of course it has, and we should admit this fact and stand against religious violence in all forms. But that is not the only question or even the most important one. Others remain:

> If religion has played a role in the violence, what precisely is that role?
>
> Is *religion* the cause of the violence, or is it an *abuse of religion* that brings about such violence?
>
> Isn't *irreligion* also the cause of great violence and cruelty?
>
> If so, then what does that indicate about the real cause of the violence?
>
> Might the cause be something different than either religion or irreligion?

These questions, and others like them, need to be addressed if we are serious about finding solutions to the problem of violence in our world.

For now, let us turn to what I take to be the most important question of all regarding the connection between religion and violence: Is there reason to believe violence, even religious violence, would disappear if religion were eradicated from the world, or might the violence continue and simply be carried out under different labels or auspices? In my view, this question is pivotal because answering it has the potential to lead us closer to the true cause or causes of violence. And if it is violence we seek to prevent, then what can be more important than doggedly pursuing its true sources? Only then can we address them.

Dawkins, Hitchens, and Harris have all argued that religion produces motivations for violence and cruelty unparalleled by other, nonreligious worldviews. A prime example of such motivators is the promise of paradise for suicide bombers. What nonreligious motivation could possibly match such an incentive? Indeed, since this promise has been splashed around the world through various news media, it is easy to see why many people have concluded that the way to stop the violence is clear: make religion disappear. But would it work?

Reasons to Believe the Violence Would Not End if Religion Were Eradicated

There are a number of reasons for thinking this is a false hope, that the violence would neither vanish nor even be appreciably diminished by the eradication of religion from the world. It is time for us to go deeper and examine them and, in the process, search for the true underlying causes of the violence.

Irreligion's Violent Record

The young Russian soldier stood out in the snowy street. At first he recoiled from the icy blast of wind that burned his ears and made his eyes water. The temperature was thirteen degrees below zero Fahrenheit, and his thin summer uniform was no help in the bitter cold. After numerous attempts by his superiors to reeducate him, this was his punishment. For the next twelve nights Ivan stood in the street outside his barracks, his commanders waiting for him to renounce his faith in God. Miraculously he did not freeze, nor did he give his superiors the answers they were waiting for. They continued to interrogate him. They put him in a refrigerated cell. They clothed him in a special rubber suit into which they pumped air until his chest was so compressed he could scarcely breathe. On July 11, 1972, Ivan wrote his parents, knowing he would soon be killed. A few days later, his body was returned to his family. He had been stabbed six times around the heart. He had wounds on his head and around his mouth and there were signs of beating on his entire body.[7]

This true story is one of many compiled by the organization Voice of the Martyrs, a group whose goal is to be a voice in the outside world for people who are quietly killed for their faith. There are many things we do not know about the young soldier in this story. Was he from a wealthy family or a poor one? Was he a good soldier or substandard? Was he popular with his fellow soldiers or a loner? Did he have a promising future as a scientist or did things look bleak? Since this story is true, there are undoubtedly answers to all these questions somewhere, but most of us will never know them. There is one thing, however—one critically important thing—that we do know about this young soldier, and that is that he had chosen to be a Christian and to publicly identify himself as such. In his case it was really all that mattered because this choice put him at odds with his government, which was ardently atheistic and was spending a good deal of money and effort getting its citizens to be as atheistic as possible. It was willing, in fact, to go to almost any length necessary to meet this goal, including inflicting brutal violence upon its citizens.

Stories like this one point up a disturbing fact that seems to escape people's notice, especially those who charge religion with breeding violence: when it comes to inflicting brutal violence on people, one of the few forces in the world that may have an even worse record than religion is irreligion. Paul Marshall, senior fellow at Freedom House's Centre for Religious Freedom in Washington, DC, and adjunct professor at the Free University of Amsterdam, has chronicled the record of violence done in the pursuit of an atheist agenda in countries around the world, and it is gruesome reading indeed.[8] He points out that with the Bolshevik Revolution of 1917, Russia adopted an atheist ideology that it later imposed on other parts of the U.S.S.R. This was the first time, says Marshall, that a state adopted the abolition of religion as official policy. This policy was not abandoned until the late 1980s, and during the intervening years the level of violence and brutality inflicted upon religious believers of all stripes was devastating. Russian Communists developed and perfected techniques of repression in order to pursue this atheist agenda, and when church leaders tried to resist, they were often imprisoned, tortured, or worse. Marshall points out that in the 1920s and 1930s alone "approximately two hundred thousand Russian Orthodox priests, monks, and nuns were slaughtered. A further half million were imprisoned or deported to

Siberia." The Russian State Commission investigating the NKVD and KGB secret police archives described the grisly treatment of religious leaders in the following words: "Most priests were shot or hanged, although other methods used by Communist death squads included crucifying pastors on their church doors [or] leaving them to freeze to death after being stripped and soaked in water during winter."[9]

In their efforts to enforce their atheist ideology, the Soviet authorities systematically eliminated and destroyed the vast majority of churches and priests during the period 1918–1941. Indeed, the history of the Soviet Union is replete with accounts of the burning and dynamiting of huge numbers of churches. The facts are unsettling to put it mildly, and the point is clear: This violence and cruelty was carried out as part of an atheist agenda. The goal was to eliminate religion, and the acts of violence and brutality in pursuit of this goal were both numerous and horrific.[10]

In China the record of violence in the pursuit of an atheist agenda was even worse. In 1949 Mao Zedong gained victory over the Nationalist Kuomintang, and with the retreat of the Kuomintang to Taiwan, he declared the establishment of the People's Republic of China. Mao's reign, which ended with his death in 1976, was characterized by brutal, massive ideological campaigns and resulted in literally millions of deaths. According to Marshall, in the 1950s Mao Zedong sought to control religion through government-controlled religious groups and the total suppression of uncooperative religious leaders through brutal labor camps, murder, or exile.[11]

Lest we are tempted to think the violence was motivated by something other than a pursuit of an anti-religious agenda, it is important to understand the way Mao carried out his program. Religious believers were called upon to accept the priority of communism—a purely secular ideology at least in Mao's version of it—over their own faith. Those who refused were labeled *counter-revolutionaries* and sentenced to twenty years or more in prison or labor camps. Especially from 1955 forward, the government strove to eliminate counter-revolutionaries from the church. Clergy were arrested, given lengthy prison sentences, and treated viciously in China's "reeducation through labor" camps.

In the 1960s and 1970s Mao went even further and closed all places of worship in an attempt to extinguish religion altogether. The point is that communism was held to be supreme and, therefore, religion was viewed as a threat. Paul Marshall describes the magnitude and horrific nature of the violence done against religious believers during this period.

> In the Cultural Revolution from 1966 to 1976, probably tens of millions of people were killed and tens of millions more disgraced. In this period, the Red Guards were particularly brutal with China's believers, whether Christian, Muslim, or Buddhist. It was perhaps the largest intense persecution of Christians in history. The level of atrocity that took place during that epoch is beyond comprehension.[12]

Marshall cites one particularly shameful act against a mother and her son as an example of the way religious believers were treated: "In one incident a mother and son were tortured, buried alive atop one another in a single grave, then dismembered and eaten by their tormentors. There were thousands of participants in mass cannibalism. The climate was gruesome madness."[13]

Paul Marshall reports that since Mao's death in 1976, the Chinese government has tolerated some religious expression but only within government-registered organizations. Reports of violence in many forms against religious believers continue to come out of this country. These include arrests, fines, imprisonments, economic discrimination, torture, restrictions on sermon content, "reeducation" in labor camps, destruction of places of worship, and even death.[14]

We have not mentioned similar documented acts of violence done against people of faith in such countries as Vietnam, North Korea, or Romania. In Russia and China alone, as we have seen, tens of millions of religious believers have been subjected to horrific violence, and the point we dare not miss is that there has not been even a hint of religious motivation behind this violence. Indeed, it is irreligion—specifically atheism and the desire to remove all threats to atheistic communism—that has been the motivating factor behind the brutality.

We should not miss the point here. In terms of sheer numbers, the violence done in the pursuit of irreligious agendas may well exceed anything ever done in the name of religion. We must ask again: Could it be that the only thing worse than religion in breeding violence in our world is irreligion?

These facts are so evident and beyond refutation that even the new critics of religion do not try to contest them. How, then, do they respond? Richard Dawkins, who states that he is presented with these facts at the end of every public lecture, readily agrees that nonreligious people, including atheists, are guilty of committing acts of violence, but he argues that there is no logical pathway from irreligion to violence as there is from religion to violence. In other words, irreligion is not the *cause* of the violence per se; it's just that some acts of violence have been brought about by people who happen to be irreligious. Their irreligion did not motivate them to carry out the violence.

> What matters is not whether Hitler and Stalin were atheists, but whether atheism systematically *influences* people to do bad things. There is not the smallest evidence that it does. . . . Stalin was scathing about the Russian Orthodox Church, and about Christianity and religion in general. But there is no evidence that his atheism motivated his brutality. . . . Individual atheists may do evil things but they don't do evil things in the name of atheism.[15]

It is an interesting approach to an uncomfortable set of facts for Dawkins: admit the violence but deny it has been carried out *because of* atheism or irreligion. Unfortunately, this approach accomplishes less than he seems to think for two reasons: First, even if he is right that violent acts such as those chronicled above were not motivated by atheism or irreligion, this response amounts to an important admission. It recognizes that violence, in fact a great amount of violence, has been inflicted by people who had no religious agenda whatsoever. But this means that the great hope of ending or even seriously reducing violence by getting rid of religion is a false hope. For all we know, violence might increase if religion were eliminated since the Stalins and Maos of the world might then inflict brutalities on people associated with other perceived threats to their ideologies. In any case, Dawkins's own reply shows there is no reason to believe violence would cease to be a serious problem in our world. The fact that these perpetrators of violence were not religious did not hold them back in the slightest from inflicting it in great quantities on their unfortunate victims. The highly significant implication of this fact is that it looks very much like neither *religion* nor *the lack of religion* is at the heart of the problem of violence in our world. Brutality has been inflicted in vast quantities by people, religious or not, and it looks suspiciously like the real cause is deeper.

But second, we must ask on what basis Dawkins can deny that irreligious people have carried out violence *because* of their irreligion. This notion appears utterly baseless, especially given the facts we saw above. Mao, Stalin, and others targeted religious leaders, believers, and places of worship precisely because religion was seen as a threat to the atheistic ideology they were following. It simply lacks credibility to argue that there is no logical pathway between this atheistic ideology and the acts of violence carried out in pursuit of the ideology.

So if violence is perpetrated both by religious and nonreligious people and the real cause of it is deeper than either religion or irreligion, then what is this cause or causes? Answering this question will lead us to our second reason for believing that the violence would not disappear or even be seriously reduced if religion were eliminated.

Political Causes of Religious Violence

In the past decade a flood of media reports has highlighted the religious beliefs of the perpetrators of a number of well-known acts of terror. It is no surprise, then, that many people have come to simply take it for granted that religion is the cause of this violence. But as has been shown by Robert Pape, professor of political science at the University of Chicago and a specialist in international security affairs, this conclusion is simplistic and misses a number of important facts. In his carefully researched 2005 account of the motivations and causes of suicide attacks, including research on every suicide bombing since 1980, he shows that we are too hasty if we believe religious motivations are all there is to it. In a nutshell, actions that appear at face value to be instances of *religious* violence, pure and simple, such as suicide missions, often have deeper *political* motivations. Religious belief, he argues, is neither *necessary* nor *sufficient* to move people to commit suicide attacks. In other words, suicide missions may occur with no religious motivation whatsoever, and even when religion does play a part, it is never enough in itself to bring about the attacks. The fundamental motivation is political, says Pape, and it would remain regardless of whether religion played a part or not. Normally the political motivation consists of the desire to force the withdrawal of some occupying foreign force from one's land by people who feel oppressed yet have insufficient military resources to fight a conventional war.[16]

This political desire to evict an oppressor is sometimes joined with a religious element, and sometimes it is not. When it is, religion becomes a handy tool to press young men into service to carry out acts of terrorism. This is a topic about which we will say more later, but the important fact, says Pape, is that these acts would be carried out with or without the religious element.

Pape's analysis is both striking and realistic, and it should give us all pause to think deeply about what is behind so-called religious violence. By way of example, how many of us truly believe that the same number of suicide attacks would have been carried out by young Arab men against British and American targets over the past few years if Israel did not exist or did not exist where it does with British and American support or if United States troops had not been stationed in Saudi Arabia? A moment's thought makes clear how preposterous such a notion would be. I ask this not to question the legitimacy of Israel's existence or the support given to it by America or other nations but only to remind us that, as Pape has shown, the causes of the violence are fundamentally political, not religious.

His analysis is borne out by a statement made by none other than Osama bin Laden in a videotape from October 2001, barely one month after the 9/11 attacks. In his message he spoke of the "humiliation and disgrace" Islam had suffered for "more than eighty years." As Robert Louis Wilken, professor of the history of Christianity at the University of Virginia, has pointed out, few Westerners caught the allusion, but bin Laden's Muslim listeners understood his reference at once. They were aware of certain events in history that most Westerners were not. In 1918 the Ottoman Empire was defeated by the Allies, and its Arabic-speaking provinces were divided up by the Western powers in a way that suited their interests. They were even given new names by Britain and France. As if that was not enough, a few years later the Turks succeeded in liberating the Turkish-speaking parts of the empire, mainly modern Turkey, and then Turkish leader Ataturk promptly established a secular state whose laws on religion were influenced by Western practices. The final straw came in 1922, roughly eighty years before 9/11, when Ataturk abolished the caliphate, an institution that was the symbol of Islamic glory and that reached back to the very beginning of Islamic history. With its destruction went the ideal of a single Muslim community bound together by political and religious authority. It also inaugurated a period of unprecedented hegemony of Western power and influence as well as severe humiliation for the Islamic world since it now perceived itself to be under the thumb of Western imperialistic powers in its own homeland.[17]

The point is that even bin Laden acknowledged that the fundamental motivation behind the attacks of 9/11 was political and not merely religious. And that is the point we dare not miss. Powerful political motivations stand behind many acts of so-called religious violence in our world, and any serious assessment of the issue must take these into account.

But *political* motivations behind violent acts do not stand alone. There are also *cultural* motivations, which may be even more powerful than political ones. If we are to get to the bottom of why people carry out acts of violence, we must understand how people's commitment to their culture sometimes moves them to such acts, and it is to this question that we now turn.

Cultural Causes of Religious Violence

In his magnificent book *Reconciling the Solitudes*, philosopher Charles Taylor points out something that should be obvious. Humans need community, and most of us know it. Our communities, or cultures, and the values we are taught through them provide meaning for our lives. They enable us to answer the deepest questions of life such as: Who am I? What is of the highest value? What is truly significant? What is most moving? What is beautiful? Taylor goes so far as to assert that no person could function as a truly human subject if he remained outside of a community that provides values, allegiances, and the like. For this reason, none of us are likely to give up our culture and values easily.[18]

This insight has great importance for our study. It explains why people rise up and take action, sometimes violently, to fend off perceived threats to their culture. Taylor's example of this phenomenon is the French-Canadian culture in Quebec, which has a history of feeling threatened by the much larger English culture of Canada surrounding it. The terrorist acts of the FLQ (Front de libération du Québec) triggered the October Crisis in the province of Quebec in 1970. The kidnapping of British trade commissioner James Cross, the demand for ransom money and release of political prisoners, the kidnapping and eventual murder of Quebec labour minister Pierre Laporte, and the martial law invoked by Canada's prime minister Pierre Trudeau to respond to this crisis amply illustrate the willingness to use violence and terrorism to defend one's culture.[19]

Notice that religion played no part in this violence. It was motivated purely by the desire to fend off a perceived threat to their cultural values and heritage. As recently as December 2007, Quebec's separatist party, the Parti Quebecois (PQ), officially called on the government of Canada to enshrine the predominance of French, and the "fundamental values of the Quebec nation," in the provincial Charter of Rights. In the words of PQ leader Pauline Marois, "It's important for us to affirm our values so it's not ambiguous when someone comes to live in this place, Quebec."[20]

Other examples of cultural groups using violence to protect their culture and values are easy to find. In 1990 members of Canada's First Nations people were involved in a protest in Kanehsatake, Quebec, over plans to expand a golf course onto land claimed by them. This led to a violent standoff lasting seventy-eight days with Mohawk warriors holding off provincial police, townspeople, and the military. The standoff, now known as the Oka Crisis, culminated in a police raid on July 11, 1990, on Mohawk barricades at the Akwesasne reserve near Oka, Quebec.[21]

For the entire seventy-eight days of this crisis, one particularly prominent Mohawk warrior, Ronald Cross (better known by his code name, Lasagna) captured the media's and thus the world's attention by his masked face, combat fatigues, and bellicose manner. As the standoff continued, he came to symbolize the whole affair, becoming a hero to his supporters in the process. To them he served as a testament to the fierce spirit of First Nations people everywhere. And what did he do that turned him into a hero? He defended the cultural heritage and way of life of his people. This is the stuff of which heroes are sometimes made.[22]

This raises the far more important question of whether this same desire to ward off cultural threats might be behind some of the recent acts of religious terrorism with which we have become all too familiar. John C. Zimmerman of the University of Nevada, Las Vegas, an expert both in demographics regarding the holocaust and in recent acts of Islamic terrorism, argues that an honest analysis of these recent acts reveals precisely this desire as the primary motivation behind most of them. In particular, when it comes to the mother of all acts of terrorism, 9/11, Zimmerman asserts that if we are to understand this horrific day, two sets of causes must be noted. The first and immediate cause was the *political* motivation we have outlined above, namely Osama bin Laden's and the radical Islamist objection toward United States troops in Saudi Arabia. The second cause was the *cultural* one with which we are concerned here, namely the long-term desire to fend off the threat to their culture that bin Laden and others believed had been coming from the West for many years.

The eminent historian of Islam, Bernard Lewis, has confirmed this motivation and explains it further by noting that for Al-Qaeda "it is the seduction of America and of its profligate, . . . dissolute way of life that represents the greatest threat to the kind of Islam they wish to impose on their fellow Muslims."[23] Bin Laden's own statements after the 9/11 attacks illustrate his motivation for orchestrating them. In October 2002, one year after 9/11, he denounced American culture as "the worst civilization witnessed in history" and called upon Americans themselves "to reject the immoral acts of fornication, homosexuality, intoxicants, gambling and usury."[24]

Nor is bin Laden the first Arab leader to feel this way. Far from it. The long-term desire among Arabs to ward off the threat to their culture from the West is well documented. The very existence of the Muslim Brotherhood, a group founded by Hasan al-Banna in 1928 with the express purpose of undoing the dangerous influence of Western culture, bears witness to this desire. Al-Banna spoke of a wave of atheism and lewdness coming from the West and engulfing Egypt. He was also greatly disturbed by what he saw in Turkey with the rise of Kemal Ataturk, the Turkish leader who began to enact Western-style reforms in the 1920s, since they too represented an attack on their cultural values.

In al-Banna's mind, Western culture was profoundly defective. It represented technical know-how and economic progress, but he declared that it was "not able to give the human soul a ray of light, a hint of inspiration or a strand of faith. It was not able to provide any means of peace and tranquility for anxious souls. . . . Indeed all that Western life could offer [a person] was material pleasure: an excess of wealth, sex and other corrupted vices, with which he temporarily indulges himself, only to find that he is not satisfied." In the West, al-Banna found "unlimited pleasure seeking, enjoyment, meanness of nature; lowliness . . . and a destructive leaning towards the things which are most damaging to wisdom and body."[25]

The real problem for bin Laden, al-Banna, and others has always been that this deficient culture has never remained in the West. It would be one thing for it to stay there and wreak its corruptive effects on people unfortunate enough to come under its influence. But it has not. Instead, Western culture has continually been exported around the world, and the results of the cultural invasion were seen by the presence of seminude women, liquor, theaters, ballrooms, magazines, and the like growing up within Islamic cultures. The worst part was that many Muslims, including some influential ones, were drawn in by these seductive influences. The effect has been seeds of doubt and disbelief in the minds of some Muslims who then began to criticize their own people and way of life and to yearn for a more Western lifestyle. This trend has been deeply distressing to people like Hasan al-Banna and Osama bin Laden. In their view, their entire culture and way of life is being destroyed.

Egyptian writer and activist Sayyid Qutb, who lived from 1906 to 1966 and greatly influenced bin Laden and current Al-Qaeda ideology, spoke in dramatic terms of the threat to his culture posed by the decadence of the West. He grimly declared that it was characterized by "material prosperity, sensual enjoyment and sexual satisfaction [which] lead to a sinking into the morass of nervous and psychological disease, sexual perversion, constant anxiety, illness, lunacy, frequent crime and the lack of . . . human dignity in life."[26] In his words, America and the West represent "an overwhelming danger to humanity. . . . Should we not issue a sentence of death?"[27]

This message was acted on very publicly by Iran's infamous leader Ayatollah Khomeini, who will go down in history as one of the most vitriolic Islamist critics of the evils of Western culture and the threat he believed they posed to his own culture and way of life. Sweeping to power in 1979, he immediately pointed an accusing finger at the West and was specific about where its flaws lay. In an interview with Italian journalist Qriana Fallaci, he said, "We are not afraid of your science and of your technology. We are afraid of your ideas and of your customs." He explained this fear by observing that imported foreign goods caused his people to be preoccupied with luxury items that, he said, pitted people and families against each other. This caused "the attraction of our youth . . . to prostitution and places for that purpose," and, if allowed to continue, he had no doubt it would lead to the ruin of the youth. But Khomeini went further, actually viewing certain Western values, such as the separation of church and state, as conspiracies aimed at the Islamic world.[28] When he seized power in 1979, he reversed the perceived evils of Westernization in Iran that had been allowed by the Shah and struck out against America by kidnapping personnel from the American embassy and holding them captive for 444 days.

The upshot is that just as we saw with First Nations people throughout North America and the FLQ in Quebec, the view that violent acts by Muslims around the world are driven by religion alone turns out, indeed, to be too simple. The real driving forces behind these acts are underlying political and cultural concerns—a fact that also helps explain why violence is carried out in troubling quantities by both religious and irreligious people around the world. It also explains the fact that when acts of religious violence are carried out, they are condemned by the vast majority of religious people. Religion is not the primary driver of the violence after all, which means that the hope of ending the violence by eliminating religion is a false one.

One complicating factor should be addressed, namely the very notion of Islamic culture. We have argued that many acts of violence carried out by Muslims that appear to be religiously motivated are actually driven primarily by the desire to defend their culture. But isn't religion an integral part of their culture? In other words, aren't cultural motives really religious motives as well in this case? If so, it would follow that when Muslims defend their culture they are also defending their religion. This would mean that religion is playing a larger role after all.

It is important to note, however, that religion has played a role in the building of virtually all cultures around the world—sometimes larger and other times smaller. Wherever we find people, we normally find religious beliefs of some kind, and these beliefs influence people's behaviors and values, and thus the formation of their cultures. We must not lose sight, however, of the fact that when we refer to a culture—any culture—we mean far more than its religious beliefs and practices. We refer to an entire way of living and thinking that has been shaped by many factors, one of which is usually religion. And this is also true of Islamic cultures. They too constitute entire ways of living and thinking that have been influenced, in part, by Islamic religious teachings. When Muslims feel their culture is threatened by influences from the West, it is this entire way of life, the overall culture, that is perceived to be under threat, not merely their religious teachings.

The point is that *religious* motives alone are not adequate to explain acts of so-called religious violence. There are also underlying *cultural* and *political* incentives driving people to protect their culture and way of life from perceived threats, and in a number of Islamic cultures, the perceived threat is enormous and comes from Western influences that are seen as powerful, seductive, insidious, and immoral. To counter it, certain members are rising up in the most effective ways they have at their disposal to strike back at the source of the threat—America and her allies.

Let us recall Charles Taylor's analysis that revealed how important cultural values are to all of us. They allow us to function as human beings by giving our lives meaning and providing the necessary framework within which we can answer life's most basic questions. It is no wonder, then, that people sometimes take fierce measures to protect their cultural values.

This raises a question: If violent acts that appear on the surface to be religiously motivated are really caused by political and cultural factors, does this mean religion plays no part whatsoever in the violence? One could be tempted to draw this conclusion, but this also turns out to be too simple. Anyone who hears the testimonies of suicide bombers or of those who have destroyed abortion clinics will quickly realize that religion sometimes plays a role in their motives and actions. This fact is undeniable. The more difficult challenge is determining what, precisely, this role is and how it relates to the deeper political and cultural causes we have considered.

Religion's Role in the Violence

Given the seriousness of the charges brought against religion that we discussed at the beginning of this book, it is hard to imagine a more important task than determining religion's precise role in the violence. How does one go about such a task, especially in the light of the facts we have seen? Both religious and irreligious people commit acts of violence, and when they occur, the vast majority of religious people around the world are outraged by them, regardless of whether they are committed in the name of religion. Furthermore, these acts are often driven by deeper political and cultural motivations. What part, then, does religion play in it all?

British theologian and philosopher Alister McGrath's suggestion is well worth considering. Religion, he says, has often been the perfect tool available to press young people (yes, they are almost always young) into performing "acts of service" to aid in the struggle against powers that pose a threat, whether political or cultural. It is not difficult to see the awesome power of religion's influence when used this way. These acts of service are often performed at great personal expense—even death—to the one carrying out the action. But what is that compared to the promise of unimaginable eternal rewards that religion offers?

When used this way, religion becomes vile. It has the ominous power to radically change the normal human conflicts that societies have always endured into cosmic battles in which the will and authority of a divine being are invoked. When this happens, the conflict becomes not merely one of good versus evil—a common premise underlying most conflicts and wars—but one of God versus the infidels, and devoted followers of God can usually be found to carry out God's will on earth. When the conflict is framed in these terms, the normal constraints and rational explanations for solving human conflicts lose their effect, and religion becomes an effective ally for those wanting to fight their political and cultural battles.[29]

All Ideals Can Be Abused

This constitutes a horrific abuse of religion. We should remember, however, that religion is not the only ideal that can be abused and turned to evil purposes. Other alternatives exist such as liberty, equality, nationalism, community, tolerance, and even atheism, as we have seen. When a society becomes secularized, it tends to elevate some alternative, nonreligious ideal to the level of what Alister McGrath calls "quasi-divine authorities" that none are permitted to challenge. He cites the familiar example of Madame Rolande.

During the French Revolution the traditional notions of God were discarded as obsolete and replaced by other ideals, most notably liberty and equality, which were then elevated to this quasi-divine status. In 1792 Madame Rolande was brought to the guillotine to face execution on trumped-up charges. As she awaited her death, she bowed mockingly to the statue of liberty and uttered the words: "Liberty, what crimes are committed in your name."[30]

Indeed, as Gwynne Dyer, war historian, defense and foreign policy analyst, and former professor at the Royal Military Academy Sandhurst, has written in his magnificent history of warfare entitled *War*, the entire French Revolution (1789–1815) was an exercise in capitalizing on a new, widespread commitment to the two great, secular principles of liberty and equality. These ideals were used to motivate 2.4 million soldiers to fight bloody battles across Europe—battles that in the end caused the deaths of over four million people. The goal of the revolution was to establish French domination over all of Europe and, in effect, create a world empire. As Dyer shows, the principles of liberty and equality made it all possible, even though in the end the ultimate goal was not accomplished.

> The French Revolution, with its principles of liberty and equality, first stimulated and then exploited a fervent nationalism that made con-

scription acceptable. It also made French troops behave differently. [It] produced soldiers who had the loyalty and initiative to fight in more open and mobile formations . . . less likely to desert and so numerous that a few desertions mattered less.[31]

Notice there was not a hint of religious motivation for this new and fervent nationalism, this openness to conscription that meant millions of young men were shipped off to fight wars in other lands, and this new kind of soldier who was willing to fight openly and less likely to desert. The driving force for all of these was a commitment to two entirely secular principles: liberty and equality, which in turn produced a fiery nationalism.

We dare not miss the significance of this, especially in the light of the fact that the bloodiness of the revolution was unparalleled in its day. The restricted warfare of the eighteenth century and before was forever lost as a result of the French Revolution.[32] Entire populations were mobilized for war, giving generals resources on a scale previously unheard of. Furthermore, the battles of the French Revolution and the Napoleonic Wars were fiercer, larger, and far more numerous than previous ones. On average, battles were fought more than once a week on one or another of the several fronts where campaigns were in progress. Few of the troops, once conscripted, were ever released again as long as they were still physically able to fight, and when the empire ended in 1815 with the defeat at the Battle of Waterloo, fewer than half of them returned home. As Napoleon once famously said, "Troops are made to get killed." When it all ended with the Battle of Waterloo, at least four million people had died, and it all occurred with no religious motivation whatsoever.[33]

The plain fact is that due to human nature, all ideals, however wonderful they start out, are capable of being abused. Since this is so, we need to figure out what to do about it rather than simply lashing out at one of those ideals—religion—as if it were the true cause of the violence. Doing that makes as little sense as lashing out at liberty and equality because of the horrendous consequences of their abuse during the French Revolution. This misses the mark and leaves the root problem untouched.

Finding and addressing that root problem should be the aim of everyone concerned about the rising violence in our world, whether religious or not. More will be said about the root cause as this book unfolds, but it is clear that if we hope to find it we must turn our attention to what may be the most foundational question of all: Why do human beings divide into groups in the first place? We do so in many ways, and these divisions and groupings provide the soil from which conflict and violence often arise. Without them, the amount of violence in the world would be greatly reduced because most of it is directed at members of one group by those of another. And since most of these divisions are unrelated to religion, it is one more reason to believe the violence would not be stopped by simply eliminating religion. It is to this reason we now turn.

Sociological Causes of Human Divisions

Consider the vast number of ways we divide ourselves up: families, nationalities, ethnicities, tribes, various religious identities, clubs, gangs, countries, and nations, to name a few. Why so many divisions? Why any at all? As sociologists point out, these divisions are social constructs we create because of our deep need for communities. We have already noted the profound benefits of community, which range from giving us identity, value, and meaning to helping us answer our deepest questions about life. With all these benefits, however, we may overlook the fact that these same communities have another effect upon us, one that often produces strife and conflict. They lead us to define and identify other people as either inside or outside our groups. Those inside are friends and comrades with whom we have deep commonalities. All others are enemies, or at least outsiders.

Thus this *binary opposition*, as it is called, helps shape our perceptions both of ourselves and others. It leads to the category of the *other*, namely the devalued half of a binary opposition. In fact, defining the *other* in a particular way is often an effective means of enhancing one's own group identity.[34]

The profound effects of these divisions and perceptions have become blatantly obvious in recent years. For this reason, the nature and function of binary opposition has been the subject of important studies. One recent, noteworthy debate between competing schools of thought has centered on whether these binary oppositions shape and determine the way people think or are themselves the products of human thought patterns. Fortunately there is no need to settle that question here. What is important is that while this binary opposition is sometimes defined in *religious* terms—as in Protestant versus Catholic, believer versus infidel, or Shiite versus Sunni—most often the definitions are entirely *nonreligious* and are framed in terms of ethnicity, tribe, language, nationality, shared interests, or even gender, age, sexual orientation, or political views.[35]

The story of the Rwandan genocide in 1994 serves as a graphic example of *tribal* divisions that led to bloody violence. Long-term hostility and fear between Hutus and Tutsis in that country, inflamed by a civil war and the suspicious death of Hutu president Juvenal Habyarimana, gave rise to a situation in which Hutus were given the order via radio to kill as many Tutsis as they could. Tutsis were vilified, labeled as cockroaches, and treated as filth to be cleaned off the streets. One such message heard on the Hutu radio station RTLM (Radio-Télévision Libre des Mille Collines) was particularly vivid: "Kill! Kill! Go to Nyamirambo! I have just been there, and there aren't any bodies in the streets yet. It's still tidy. You have to start cleaning!"[36]

And they did. The death toll was over eight hundred thousand people who were hacked to death by machete or killed in other similarly gruesome ways. The violence resulting from these tribal divisions was overwhelming. It will go down in history as a human tragedy of historic proportions, and one that had very little, if anything, to do with religion.

It is simply naïve to think getting rid of religion would bring about an end of, or even a significant reduction in, human divisions or the conflicts to which they frequently lead. Such thinking ignores the fundamental fact that we humans will inevitably create communities to satisfy our deep need for self-identity and belonging. If religion were eliminated, other group identifiers would emerge and communities would continue to be formed. Unfortunately, the resulting binary opposition and devaluing of outsiders, which prepares the ground out of which violence often arises, would also occur.

By now it should be clear that identifying the true cause or causes of religious violence is a more complex matter than merely pointing the finger at religion as if eliminating it would somehow make the violence cease. The facts speak for themselves, and a few of the most significant ones are worth reiterating:

1. Both religious and irreligious people commit acts of violence.
2. When they occur, the vast majority of religious people around the world are outraged by them regardless of whether they are committed in the name of religion.
3. These acts are often driven by deep political and cultural motivations that would remain regardless of whether religion played a part.

4. Religion is sometimes turned into a tool to help recruit soldiers to fight these political and cultural battles.
5. While this is a horrific abuse of religion, virtually any ideal can be abused, including secular ones such as liberty and equality.
6. Humans will always divide into communities, resulting in divisions and binary oppositions that lie at the heart of human conflict. Some of these divisions are religious in nature, but most are not.

These facts show that we are on the wrong track if we think eliminating religion would end or even seriously diminish violence in our world, even so-called religious violence. This means something deeper than religion lies at the heart of the problem, and finding this root cause should be the goal of everyone concerned about this heartbreaking problem in our world.

But for those who persist in arguing that religion is the culprit in causing violence, this charge does not stand alone. As we noted earlier, it is closely connected to the sister charge that religion, by its very nature, is irrational and causes people to believe irrational ideas. The allegation is that some of these irrational religious beliefs are leading people to commit horrific acts of violence. Worse yet, since such charges are evidence-free, there is no way to dissuade people from believing or acting on them. Thus the charges of *violence* and *irrationality* in religion come together. Having responded to the first of these, it is now time to turn our attention to the second.

4

Is Christianity Irrational and Devoid of Evidence?

What are we to make of the charge that religion is an irrational phenomenon that "float[s] entirely free of reason and evidence"? How can we reply to Sam Harris, who argues that while religious people tend to be as reasonable or rational as anyone else in the rest of their lives, they treat their religious lives entirely differently?[1] Recall his statement, quoted earlier, that highlights this perceived compartmentalization in religious people:

> Tell a devout Christian that his wife is cheating on him or that frozen yogurt can make a man invisible and he is likely to require as much evidence as anyone else. . . . [However] tell him that the book he keeps by his bed was written by an invisible deity who will punish him . . . for eternity if he fails to accept its every incredible claim about the universe, and he seems to require no evidence whatsoever.[2]

The willingness to believe religious ideas that are neither rational nor based on evidence has produced a dangerous situation in the world, says Harris. Not only are beliefs like this immune from persuasion, but some of them are creating a willingness to commit violent acts. So we must ask: Are religious beliefs really this irrational and dangerous?

While part of my response will apply to religion as a whole, I write as a Christian and thus am primarily concerned about whether Christianity falls victim to these allegations. There are two initial questions that arise from this charge: (1) What qualifies a belief or idea as rational or irrational, reasonable or unreasonable? (2) Is it really true that religious, or specifically Christian, claims are irrational and "float entirely free of reason and evidence," as critics like Sam Harris contend? In other words, is this allegation true of Christianity? We will begin by turning our attention to these two questions before going on to address a number of other elements of the charge of irrationality leveled by the critics.

What Does It Mean to Be Rational?

Our question here is: What exactly qualifies a belief to be rational, and what, precisely, is the flaw the critics are ascribing to religious belief when they label it as irrational? This question is almost never asked, which is interesting given how passionately and repeatedly the charge of irrationality is leveled at religious belief. Does believing in a rational manner mean limiting our beliefs to ideas that are commonly accepted? If so, how commonly? Does it mean being honest and responsible in our pursuit of truth? Does it mean demonstrating a willingness to have our ideas stand up to philosophical scrutiny? Or could it mean producing ideas that secure the support of respected men and women who display sound, rational decision making elsewhere in their lives?

Could it be that all of these supposed criteria of rationality are on the wrong track and that being rational requires that one believe only ideas for which one has evidence? If so, what kind of evidence counts, and how much of it do we need in order to cross the line from believing irrationally to believing rationally? Must the evidence be open and convincing to everyone? If not everyone, to whom and how many, and who decides this? And could there be evidence that is open to some people but not to everyone?

Or might we be mistaken to equate *evidence* with *rationality*? Certainly many philosophers who have looked into these questions think so. Evidentialism, the view that holds that a belief is rationally justified or acceptable only if it is held on the basis of good evidence, has been rejected by many in the field of epistemology, in which such questions are probed deeply, and this rejection is for good reasons.

The fact is that for all our talk about evidence, most of us would have a difficult time producing evidence for many of the things we believe and take for granted. We have neither the time nor the resources to track down such evidence, so we simply accept most of our beliefs on the word of others or because we heard them in news reports or documentaries, read them in books, or received them from other sources of information. Are we acting irrationally for holding beliefs in this way? It hardly seems so.

Furthermore, even when we do have solid evidence for certain beliefs, that evidence itself rests on other evidence, which in turn rests on still other evidence, and so on; you get the picture. Eventually we reach ground zero where we find beliefs that themselves do not rest on evidence. We accept them as our bedrock assumptions in life and work from there. This means that even the most ardent evidentialist accepts certain foundational beliefs without evidence.

In other words, for all its value in helping us search for the truth, evidence has clear limitations and, for this reason, some philosophers suggest a different approach. American philosopher and former head of the American Philosophical Association Alvin Plantinga suggests different criteria for rationality in our beliefs. He argues convincingly that for a belief to be rational, it needs to be the product of rational faculties that are functioning properly in an environment well suited to them. So long as people's rational faculties are not dysfunctional in some way—for example, in a state of confusion, bipolar disorder, delusion, or some other way—then the products of their contemplation and beliefs must be seen as rational. They are within their rights, rationally speaking, in holding these beliefs.[3] Plantinga has gained a wide hearing for his views on the rationality of belief.

Of course I am only touching the tip of the iceberg of what qualifies a belief to be rational, but that is precisely the point I wish to make at the outset. The question of what turns an irrational belief into a rational one, or vice versa, is a large one, and there is no universally agreed-upon answer to it. Furthermore, so far as I can tell, neither Harris, Dawkins, nor Hitchens have so much as attempted to provide us with clear criteria for what qualifies an idea or belief as rational. Their argument, or should I say assertion, largely consists of identifying certain beliefs held by religious people that they themselves do not believe nor could ever imagine believing and then, with a look of bewilderment, asking how anyone else could possibly believe such things either.

Beyond that, the closest any of them come to actually telling us what makes religious beliefs irrational is to assert repeatedly that certain beliefs they regard as irrational are devoid of evidence—the implication being that this is what makes them irrational. Throughout their writings, the critics speak often of the requirement of evidence for our beliefs and assert that Christianity does not meet this requirement. Notwithstanding the limitations of evidence we have noted above, it is time for us to ask our second question: Do Christian claims float free of reason and evidence?

The Assertion That Christian Beliefs "Float Entirely Free of Reason and Evidence" Is False

The most important thing we can say to the assertion that Christian truth claims "float entirely free of reason and evidence" is that it is simply false. In fact, it is so flagrantly false that one wonders what the critics are reading or researching when they make such an assertion. As many of them know, Christian philosophers and theologians such as St. Thomas Aquinas, Blaise Pascal, C. S. Lewis, Richard Swinburne, Alvin Plantinga, William Lane Craig, James P. Moreland, and a host of others throughout the history of Christianity have piled up thousands of pages of evidence for the truth claims Christianity presents to the world.

Nor can this evidence be glibly set aside as weak or unconvincing. C. S. Lewis, one of the most brilliant thinkers and writers in the English world in recent times, wrote that he rejected atheism and became a Christian not because he wanted to believe but because, to his chagrin, he found that his inquiry into the truth of Christian claims put him in touch with evidence so convincing that he had no choice but to believe. He referred to himself as the most dejected and reluctant convert in England. It is worth reading his own deeply honest description of the agony he went through before finally giving in to the evidence and embracing Christ.

> You must picture me alone in that room in Magdalen, night after night, feeling, whenever my mind lifted even for a second from my work, the steady, unrelenting approach of Him whom I so earnestly desired not to meet. That which I had greatly feared had at last come upon me. In the Trinity Term of 1929 I gave in, and admitted that God was God, and knelt and prayed: perhaps, that night, the most dejected and reluctant

convert in all England. . . . The Prodigal son at least walked home on his feet. But who can duly adore that Love which will open the high gates to a prodigal who is brought in kicking, struggling, resentful, and darting his eyes in every direction for a chance to escape?[4]

Either the new critics have not seen the evidence presented by Christian writers or they have not noticed its significance for their charge that Christian truth claims float free of evidence. Nor have they read the New Testament record of Jesus giving his disciples, the future leaders of the new movement he was founding, "many convincing proofs" that he had risen from the dead (Acts 1:3 NIV). Clearly Jesus understood the importance of providing evidence for our beliefs. He wants his disciples to be aware of good reasons for believing something as astonishing as the message that Christ has died but then risen from the dead.

The apostle Peter follows Jesus's pattern and urges his readers to always be ready to give a reason for the hope they have (1 Peter 3:15). Paul also continually brings forth evidence that is relevant to his specific audiences in his attempts to persuade them that Jesus is the divine Son of God. When speaking to Jews, he draws his evidence from Old Testament passages they know and trust in order to build a case that Jesus is their long-awaited Messiah. To Gentiles he refers not to the Old Testament but to their own philosophers and teachers to make his case convincing.[5]

Most importantly, the critics quite obviously have missed the fifteenth chapter of Paul's first letter to the Christians at Corinth—perhaps the most important passage of all in this regard. This chapter is devoted to Jesus's resurrection and what it means for his followers. The declaration that Jesus rose from the dead has always been the main message of Christianity to the world, and in this chapter Paul rests the entire Christian enterprise on this one historical event. Remarkably, he declares that if it did not happen, then the entire Christian story is a sham and we should all reject it. Notice his striking words to this effect:

If Christ has not been raised, your faith is futile and you are still in your sins. Then those also who have fallen asleep in Christ have perished. If for this life only we have hoped in Christ, we are of all men most to be pitied.

1 Corinthians 15:17–19

His contention here is so astounding that I'm afraid even some Christians are caught off guard by it. The entire Christian story, the whole Christian movement, rests on one historical event: the resurrection of Jesus. If this event did not happen, then the whole story is a farce and we should immediately reject it. Amazingly, this call to walk away from Christianity if Jesus did not rise comes not from an enemy of Christianity, nor even from some neutral observer, but from the very pages of the New Testament.

This shows that evidence is not an enemy of Christian faith. It is more like a natural ally since the only way to determine whether historical events, such as the resurrection of Jesus, actually happened in history is to seek out and evaluate the evidence for them. Given the supreme importance placed on Jesus's resurrection, it is no surprise that throughout the history of the Christian faith, Christian thinkers have compiled evidence for this event. In fact, in this very chapter in the New Testament (1 Corinthians 15) Paul himself gives evidence to his readers that Jesus really is raised from the dead. He mentions specific people to whom Jesus appeared alive and well after he was publicly crucified. Renowned German theologian Wolfhart Pannenberg points out that in this passage, 1 Corinthians 15:3–8, the apostle Paul is following the normal procedure used by Greek historians in his day, such as Herodotus, in proving historical events, namely the listing of witnesses.[6] In other words, using the accepted method of his day for establishing the credibility of one's claims, he names people as witnesses who were still alive and available to be questioned. One would not do that unless there were real people to back up one's claims. Even Rudolph Bultmann, no believer in Jesus's bodily resurrection, reluctantly agrees. Referring to this text in 1 Corinthians 15, he writes, "I can understand the text only as an attempt to make the resurrection of Christ credible as an objective historical fact."[7]

Beyond this evidence, Christian philosophers have pointed to a number of well-attested facts as evidence for the truth of Jesus's resurrection. These include Jesus's burial in a tomb owned by Joseph of Arimethea, who is described as a prominent member of the Jewish Sanhedrin—something of a supreme court for the Jewish people at the time—and the subsequent discovery of this tomb empty by Jesus's women followers three days later. Neither of these facts could have been fabricated. It would be too easy to do a quick fact-check to see if there was such a person as Joseph of Arimethea on the Sanhedrin and if Jesus's body really had been placed in his personal tomb.

Furthermore, given the low credibility of women's testimony in that society, a person writing a fabrication would not choose women as the primary witnesses to these highly significant events, especially when men were available to be used. Additional evidence comes from the postcrucifixion appearances of Jesus to over five hundred people; the disciples' *belief* that Jesus rose from the dead, which needs to be explained somehow; their preaching of this belief even at the risk of their own lives; and the formation and phenomenal growth of the new Christian movement in the very place where Jesus had been publicly crucified weeks earlier.

This evidence and much more has been argued at great length by Christian philosophers, and the arguments do not need to be repeated here.[8] What we must say, however, is that it is patently false to assert that Christian truth claims "float entirely free of reason and evidence" or that they are untestable. Not only are they testable, but the New Testament itself invites such testing. It goes as far as to call on its readers to reject the faith if the evidence says Jesus did not rise from the dead; come see for yourself what the evidence is for the resurrection. For this reason, much work in the area of Christian apologetics has centered on the evidence for the resurrection.

Clearly there is confusion about the relationship between faith and reason on the part of some of the new critics of religion. As we have seen, it is a rather simple task to show that evidence is not an enemy of Christian faith; it is more like an ally. Both the New Testament and Christian thinkers speak favorably of having reasons and evidence for believing Christian truth claims. No conflict between faith and reason is envisioned in this process. It seems, then, that something has gone wrong in the critics' understanding of the relationship between faith and evidence, but what is it?

The Critics' False Dilemma

My suggestion is that the critics are committing what most logic textbooks describe as a *false dilemma*. This occurs when a person falsely assumes that only two alternative ideas or courses of action exist when in reality others are available. The person then argues that because one of the two alternatives is obviously false or undesirable, there is no other choice but to accept the other one as true. The fallacy consists in falsely assuming only two options exist.

Examples are easy to come by. When a husband responds to his wife's shock over hearing he has just spent an exorbitant sum of money to buy a new stereo system by retorting, "What do you want me to do, keep on listening to that worn-out seventy-five-dollar stereo we've had for twelve years?" he has committed this fallacy. He has given an answer that assumes there are only two alternatives open to him: either buy the very expensive stereo or keep on listening to the worn-out seventy-five-dollar one. He is conveniently ignoring the fact that a third alternative exists, namely that of buying a less expensive stereo system than the one he purchased. It would cost less than the most expensive stereo but still be better than the old seventy-five-dollar one. In other words, he has created a false dilemma since a third alternative (or more) exists.

How have the critics committed this fallacy here? Consider Sam Harris's charge that religion "float[s] entirely free of reason and evidence." He explains this statement in his book *The End of Faith* by quoting a biblical definition of *faith* found in Hebrews 11:1: "Now faith is the assurance of things hoped for, the conviction of things not seen." Based on his reading of this text, he defines faith as "unjustified belief in matters of ultimate concern" and says this renders faith entirely self-justifying. He then illustrates this concept of faith as he understands it with a "conviction" that Nicole Kidman is in love with him even though he has never met her. The only evidence he has for her love is his feeling that she loves him, and he thus reasons that they must have a deep metaphysical connection. On the basis of this feeling, he decides to wait outside her house to meet her personally.[9]

The "conviction" Harris has that Nicole Kidman loves him is identified by him as faith since it is based purely on feeling, not real evidence, and this is the point he wishes to get across in this story: if we had evidence we would not have faith, at least not in the biblical sense of the term, because the very definition of faith excludes the possibility of evidence. Recall that he has already defined faith as "unjustified belief." The moment we begin to believe something on the basis of evidence, we no longer exercise faith, he thinks. It is one or the other.

So it comes down to this: we either look to *evidence* or we have *faith* in our holy books to give us the truth. To state it another way, we either consider the evidence for and against any truth claim *or* we trust our religious leaders. Only these two options exist as far as Harris is concerned, and for religious believers, the choice of where to look for the truth is an easy one.

But this is a false dilemma. A third alternative exists, and it is the one chosen by a huge number of Christians, including the Christian philosophers and theologians mentioned earlier and many others like them who have compiled thousands of pages of evidence for the truth of Christian claims. This alternative consists in examining evidence for the truth of Christian claims and being led, by that evidence, to embrace Jesus as the divine Son of God and the Old and New Testaments as the written revelation of God. Of course once a person accepts Jesus and the Scriptures in this way, their authority is deemed to be supreme. It is very much like accepting the authority of a king once we have learned, or been persuaded by good reasons, that he is indeed the king. If we discovered later that this so-called king is only an imposter, we would immediately cease to accept his authority.

In the same way, once we become persuaded that Jesus is the divine Son of God, we happily accept his teachings on all matters as true. The same principle applies to the Scriptures. This, however, does not change the fact that evidence and sound reasoning may have played an important part in leading us to believe that Jesus is indeed the divine Son of God or that the Scriptures are the words and messages of God. Nor does it change the fact we noted earlier that if Christians, to their dismay, ever learned that certain key claims about Jesus were false—such as the claim that he rose from the dead—they would no longer believe he is the divine Son of God. As we saw earlier, the New Testament itself calls us to consider and test its claims in precisely this way. If Jesus did not rise from the dead, then we are all advised *by the New Testament* to quit following him.

It is worth pointing out that the approach of testing truth claims is the way of the New Testament in general. The book of Acts reports that the Christians in the city of Berea, after hearing the apostle Paul speak to them, are nobler than his previous audiences precisely because they go home and investigate his message "to see if these things were so" (Acts 17:11). If one thing is clear, it is that Christianity is not inherently opposed to reason and evidence. These are allies, not enemies, of Christian faith.

But the critics' charge of irrationality goes further. As far as they are concerned, whatever Christians may say about their attitude toward reason and rationality, some of the actual beliefs they hold, including certain core teachings of their faith, are plainly irrational and should not be believed by anyone. While neither Dawkins, Harris, nor Hitchens have gone to the trouble of providing criteria for what defines an idea as rational or irrational, presumably it is worse to believe ideas that are irrational than merely those that lack evidence. Two such allegedly irrational beliefs deserve special responses: belief in God's existence and belief that God is a Trinity.

Is Belief in God Rational?

As we noted earlier in this book, the new critics of religion have great difficulty with the concept of the God of Christianity. As we shall see, however, disproving God's existence is harder than it may first appear. Sam Harris wonders how anyone could believe in a supposedly benevolent and all-powerful God who, nonetheless, allows 180,000 people to die in a tsunami. This is a reference to the traditional problem of evil in which the existence of a good and all-powerful God is said to be incompatible with the existence of evil; since evil exists, God cannot. This kind of God would presumably both *want* to and *be able* to eliminate all evil; so the fact that evil exists proves that God does not—or so says the argument from evil.[10]

But arguments based on the presence of suffering and evil are unsuccessful in disproving God. As heart-rending as events like these are, philosopher Alvin Plantinga has shown that they do not prove there is no God. At the very least, it is possible that God could have some good reasons for allowing a certain amount of evil in the world, and so long as this is possible, the existence of a God who is completely good and all-powerful has not been disproven. If we knew his reasons, they might be such as to exculpate him. Furthermore, even if we do not know what those reasons are, it does not follow that there are none. Plantinga explains it in the following way: "The fact that the theist doesn't know why God permits evil is, perhaps, an interesting fact about the theist, but by itself it shows little or nothing relevant to the rationality of belief in God."[11]

In other words, to prove a wholly good and all-powerful God does not exist, the atheist would somehow have to know, and show, that there are *no good reasons* such a God could have for permitting any evil. But how could we finite humans know a thing like that? The most we could know is that there are no good reasons *we can think of*. Perhaps so, but as Plantinga shows, that is nothing more than an interesting fact about us which does nothing to disprove God. Furthermore, it is eminently reasonable to think an infinite God would have reasons for certain actions that finite humans do not know. After all, even parents have reasons for doing things that their children do not, and in some cases could not, understand. Therefore, the presence of evil in the world does not disprove the existence of the Christian God.

Richard Dawkins attempts to address certain arguments for God's existence to show they are unsuccessful. In *The God Delusion* he plunges into a critique of St. Thomas Aquinas's famous *five ways*, in which he sets out five arguments for belief in God. This was probably a mistake on Dawkins's part since, as British theologian and philosopher Alister McGrath notes, he "is clearly out of his depth, and achieves little by his brief and superficial engagement with these great perennial debates."[12] He shows a lack of understanding of the purpose of Aquinas's arguments, which were to show the inner coherence of belief in God in the same way that atheistic arguments—such as Freud's projection of God as a father figure—are intended to do for atheism. Nowhere does Aquinas refer to these arguments as deductive proofs (proofs that attempt to demonstrate their conclusions with absolute certainty). Rather, his purpose is to argue that the indications of purpose and design we see in the universe can be explained on the basis of the existence of a creator God. In fact, faith in God offers a better fit with the world than atheism or naturalism, and therefore faith in God makes good sense of what we observe in the world. Ironically, as McGrath also notes, Dawkins himself uses the same approach to commend atheism elsewhere, so it is hard to see what he has to complain about in Aquinas.[13]

Given this misunderstanding of the purpose of Aquinas's arguments, it is not surprising that Dawkins's analysis of Aquinas's arguments also misses the mark. He confuses an *inductive empirical demonstration* of the coherence of belief in God and our observations of the world with a *deductive proof* of God's existence and, of course, pronounces the arguments all failures.

Dawkins goes further and argues that when it comes to the debate over the existence of God, atheists have no duty to prove their claim that God *does not* exist. Rather, he says, the burden of proof is on theists to prove that God *does* exist. He refers to something he calls a "favorite trick" of those who believe in God in which they shift the burden of proof to atheists and call upon them to prove there is no God. Dawkins admits, surprisingly easily, that this cannot be done but then insists that to ask for such a proof for atheism is absurd. No such proof is necessary. It is not up to atheists to prove God *does not* exist. It is up to theists to prove he *does*.

Why is this so? To support his contention regarding burden of proof, Dawkins refers to fictional characters such as the Tooth Fairy, Mother Goose, the Flying Spaghetti Monster of cyberspace, and even Bertrand Russell's famous Celestial Teapot. It would be absurd, he says, to call on people who do *not* believe in these fictional characters to prove their *non*-existence. The burden of proof is on those who do believe in them. Similarly, those who believe God exists are the ones who have the duty to prove he does, not the other way around. [14]

What shall we say to this line of reasoning concerning burden of proof? The first thing to make clear is that if Dawkins is implying that theists are depending on this "trick," as he calls it, to make their case rather than making arguments for God's existence, he is clearly mistaken. I say "if" because while he chastises theists for using this "trick," he is obviously aware of the famous five arguments set out by St. Thomas Aquinas. Dawkins himself has replied to them, although, as we saw, not well. In addition to Aquinas, philosophers and theologians such as C. S. Lewis, R. G. Swinburne, Alvin Plantinga, William Lane Craig, and a host of other lesser-known thinkers around the world have written thousands of pages arguing for the existence of God. For example, American philosopher and former head of the American Philosophical Association Alvin Plantinga has written an essay entitled "Two Dozen (or So) Theistic Arguments."[15]

But why should anyone think Dawkins is correct, in the first place, in thinking the burden of proof is strictly and always on the person who makes a *positive claim* (e.g., God exists) and never on those making a negative assertion (e.g., God does not exist)? The fact is that *every truth claim*, whether positive or negative, has a burden of proof, and when it comes to the question of God, clearly both theists and atheists are making truth claims. "God exists," says the theist. "He does not," replies the atheist. Both claim to tell us something important about the world. One says it has God in it; the other says it does not. It is hard to see what it is about *negative* truth claims that frees them from having to be justified or supported.

Consider what happens to Dawkins's contention when we simply substitute other illustrations in place of his fictional characters. What if a friend tells you that he or she did not believe pineapples or rhinoceroses exist or that George Washington, Winston Churchill, or Nero had never lived as real, historical figures? Suppose a friend goes further and insists that the World Trade Centers were not attacked on 9/11 and that even the Holocaust never occurred? He or she has heard of all these, of course, but refuses to believe in any of them. Suddenly things seem different. Notice, these are all negative truth claims about some state of affairs in the world. They tell us something is *not* the case and, in this sense, resemble the atheist's truth claim that there is no God. Does their negativity alone free your friend from having to give a reason for thinking they are not true? Hardly.

These examples show that the burden of proof does not hinge merely on whether an assertion is positive or negative, as Dawkins seems to assume. But why then does it seem to do just that in Dawkins's illustrations above concerning the Tooth Fairy and Mother Goose? The reason is because he has restricted his illustrations to trivial characters that were intended to be fictional in the first place and are recognized as such by anyone talking about them. He has strategically used fictional characters because his argument only works with characters such as these. No one is asking for evidence that the Tooth Fairy does not exist because no adult ever thought it did. It is not the *negativity* of the claims that releases them from needing any proof but their *triviality*. When we simply substitute normal, serious characters such as Plato, Nero, Winston Churchill, or George Washington in place of these fictional characters, it becomes clear that anyone denying the existence of these figures has a burden of proof equal to, and in some cases greater than, the person claiming they do exist.

One need only attend a formal debate between two opponents to see this. In every debate there is a resolution statement that one debater argues *for* (the positive position) and the other *against* (the negative position). Imagine a debater on the negative side declaring at the outset that he has nothing to prove since his truth claim is negative. "Nope," he announces, "the burden of proof is on her," pointing to the other debater. "After all, my position is only the negative one. It's not up to me to prove anything." The result would be great mirth and laughter in the room because every claim of knowledge, whether positive or negative, requires argument or evidence in its support, and no one gets off that easily. Even appealing to the Tooth Fairy or Mother Goose does not change this fact.

When it comes to belief in God, we are dealing with a serious truth claim that is held by billions of thoughtful and intelligent people. Huge numbers of our friends and neighbors, in fact, claim to have encountered him. Furthermore, as we noted earlier, dozens of arguments for God's existence have been set forth by philosophers in academic journals and books. The fact that certain people, such as

Dawkins and Harris, do not believe in God does not turn this serious truth claim into a trivial one, just as the denial of the Holocaust by some, even many, does not turn that truth claim into a trivial one either. Furthermore, the fact that Dawkins does not find these arguments for God convincing (assuming he has analyzed them all) tells us something about him but in no way proves there is no God. For that conclusion, there must be successful arguments for atheism.

Atheist philosopher Kai Nielsen admits this with great intellectual honesty. It is worth noticing how carefully he states this logical requirement:

> If the arguments for the existence of God are shown to be unsound, it does not *follow* that God does not exist. . . . To show that an argument is invalid or unsound is not to show that the *conclusion of the argument is false* . . . only . . . that the argument does not warrant our asserting the conclusion to be true. All the proofs of God's existence may fail, but it still may be the case that God exists. . . . In short, to show that the proofs do not work is not enough, by itself. . . . It still may be the case that there is a God."[16]

Nielsen is belaboring a point that is often missed, namely that the task of proving atheism requires arguments of its own no less than the job of proving theism. In the case of atheism, however, as we noted earlier, there is a special difficulty since proving there is no God involves proving what logicians call a *universal negative*. It requires showing that God does not exist anywhere in or out of the universe. As we asked earlier, do any of us really think we know enough about the universe to rule out the possibility that a divine being exists either in it or somewhere beyond it? Such knowledge would require omniscience. So long as our knowledge of the universe is finite, God's existence remains a possibility at the very least, and theism has not been disproven.

But even if the critics were willing to admit that belief in God is not inherently irrational, their allegations concerning the rationality of theism would not be fully answered. It is hard enough to believe a divine being *exists*, they say, but even harder to believe in the *kind of God* Christians talk about, namely a *trinitarian God*. Could anything be more absurd than the doctrine of the Holy Trinity? they wonder. This teaching is an object of derision to Richard Dawkins and other critics, so it is time for us to ask: Is the doctrine of a trinitarian God, which Christians have historically believed, irrational?

Is the Doctrine of the Trinity Irrational?

Dawkins identifies the Christian idea of a trinitarian God as a particularly irrational teaching. He ridicules it and asks, derisively, what on earth it could possibly mean to say Jesus is of the same essence or substance with God. Do we have one God in three parts, or is it three Gods in one? he wonders. Either way, he can make no sense of it.[17]

He is not the first person to struggle with understanding this doctrine. Not long ago I had a conversation with a young Muslim student at a central Canadian university who had recently arrived from Iran. His main difficulty with Christianity was this very doctrine: the Trinity. In his mind it was irrational, in fact outright contradictory.

What are we to say to people like Dawkins or this young student? Is this doctrine as silly as Dawkins makes it out to be? Is it internally contradictory, such that it would be impossible to believe it without suspending our normal rules of reasoning? After speaking with this young Muslim man for a few engaging minutes, we both walked away with some things to think about. I had a fresh understanding of a Muslim's perspective on this doctrine, and he had a brand-new suggestion to mull over, namely that while this doctrine clearly contains mystery, it is another matter entirely to show that it involves an internal contradiction—something I doubt either he or anyone else would be able to do.

Be that as it may, we might as well admit that this is not an easy teaching to understand and, perhaps, it is the first thing we should get clear. Christians do not embrace it because it is simple or easy. There is mystery here, but then why shouldn't there be? This doctrine represents the attempt to describe the infinite Creator of the universe using human language and thought categories.

Even with the mystery, however, I cannot help but wonder whether the Trinity ought to be the stumbling block it appears to be to some people. Would we really expect descriptions of an infinite God to be clear and simple all the way through? My hunch is that if it were so simple, many would object that this God looks like a human invention—an idea we humans have constructed and projected upon reality. In contrast, the doctrine of the Trinity looks very much like something no human would have thought up.

Christians accept this doctrine because they see it in a natural reading of the Bible. It teaches four propositions that, when taken together, lead us to formulate this doctrine. Those ideas are that:

1. Jesus is divine,
2. his Father is divine,
3. the Holy Spirit is divine, and yet
4. there is one God.

In this vein, American theologian Millard Erickson explains the Trinity in its most basic form when he asserts that biblical teaching is that "God is one and . . . three persons are God." This leads him, and many others, to speak of both the threeness and oneness of God.[18]

While there is mystery here, it is another matter to show this doctrine is self-contradictory. A contradiction exists when something is claimed to be *A* and to not be *A* at the same time and in the same sense. If I tell you that my friend John is six feet tall and then, a few minutes later, tell you he is *not* six feet tall, I have contradicted myself, assuming, of course, that John did not do something between my two statements to alter his height, such as change his shoes or his hairstyle.

If the doctrine of the Trinity taught that there is one God and at the same time three Gods, or that there is one person and at the same time three persons within God, it would be contradictory. It does not; it teaches that there is one God who manifests himself in three different persons.

Admittedly, it is difficult to see how the threeness and oneness of God relate to each other, but as Millard Erickson also notes, Christians are not the only ones who must retain two polarities as they function. In their attempts to explain the phenomenon of light, physicists hold both that it is waves and that it is particles of energy, and yet it cannot be both. As one physicist puts it: "On Monday, Wednesday, and Friday, we think of light as waves; on Tuesday, Thursday, and Saturday, we think of it as particles of energy."[19] I am not sure how physicists think of light on Sunday, but the point is that there are times when we cannot explain a mystery but feel compelled to acknowledge its presence.

I have found the explanation offered by C. S. Lewis in his well-known book *Mere Christianity* most helpful as a way to frame and think of God in three persons. He notes that a person living in a one-dimensional world would know straight lines and nothing more. He would have no concept of a figure or cube. A person living in a two-dimensional world would know lines and figures but would have no idea of a cube. He then goes on to say,

Now the Christian account of God involves just the same principle. The human level is a simple . . . level. On the human level one person is one being, and any two persons are two separate beings—just as, in two dimensions (say on a flat sheet of paper) one square is one figure, and any two squares are two separate figures. On the Divine level you still find personalities; but up there you find them combined in new ways which we, who do not live on that level, cannot imagine. In God's dimension, so to speak, you find a being who is three Persons while remaining one Being, just as a cube is six squares while remaining one cube. Of course we cannot fully conceive a being like that; just as, if we were so made that we perceived only two dimensions in space we could never properly imagine a cube. But we can get a sort of faint notion of it. . . . It is something we could never have guessed.[20]

The concept of the Trinity, far from being a contradictory and irrational concept, may well be the kind of idea we should expect to hear about an infinite, divine being if that being chose to reveal something of his nature to us. Furthermore, as Lewis notes, this concept is certainly not something any of us could have guessed. Rather than being a difficulty, however, this is one of the reasons he became a Christian. Once we understand it, he observes, we find that reality itself is usually not the sort of thing we would have guessed. If Christianity presented the kind of teachings about God that we would have expected, Lewis would have felt we were simply making them up. The doctrine of the Trinity, most certainly, does not appear to be a teaching anyone would have made up.

It appears, then, that the idea of the Trinity, while including mystery, is not inherently irrational after all. In fact, as Christian thinkers such as C. S. Lewis have shown, there are perfectly reasonable ways of understanding it. Furthermore, it should be clear by now that Christianity itself is neither irrational nor devoid of evidence for its truth claims. On the contrary, as we have now seen, many thoughtful and well-read Christians seek to justify their beliefs and use evidence to do so.

But one niggling question persists: Do Christians really value evidence as much as some Christians claim they do? Richard Dawkins thinks that if they do, some of them have a funny way of showing it. In *The God Delusion* he points to a statement made by renowned British theologian Richard Swinburne, which he believes tells the real story of what Christians think of evidence. It is a statement he finds both appalling and bizarre. What did Swinburne say to elicit such a strong reaction?

Could There Be Too Much Evidence?

Swinburne's offending statement was made during a discussion about the existence of God when he was asked how much evidence exists for theism. His answer, as we noted earlier in this book, was that "there is quite a lot of evidence anyway of God's existence, and too much might not be good for us."[21] Dawkins is dumbfounded by this statement. Too much evidence might not be good for us! How can too much evidence for anything be bad—especially for a claim as momentous as that God exists? As far as he is concerned, this statement betrays a bizarre and hostile attitude toward evidence itself. He is so astounded by it that he repeats it in italics and calls his readers to read it again and think about how absurd it is.

To understand Dawkins's astonishment at Swinburne's statement, it is necessary to know that Dawkins has maintained throughout his writings that the question of God's existence is not, in principle, an insurmountable problem. In *The God Delusion* he contends it could be easily settled by God himself, assuming he exists, if he simply decided to do so. He could clinch the argument noisily and unequivocally in his favor if he wanted to.[22] In Dawkins's words, "If God existed and wanted to convince us of it, he could 'fill the world with super-miracles.' "[23] No wonder then that he is astounded that anyone would claim that the very thing that could settle the matter, namely more evidence, might not be good for us. It points to a deep hostility toward evidence within religion, says Dawkins.

Why would Swinburne utter this remark? To understand it, we must see it as part of an ongoing discussion over the past few hundred years among theologians and philosophers. It is a discussion Dawkins is obviously unaware of but which he would have been wise to inquire into before voicing such incredulity. Had he done so, he would have gained some idea why a person with Swinburne's impressive credentials and achievements, something Dawkins himself alludes to, would make such a statement.

In brief, the discussion centers on the question of human freedom and the choice to believe in God. In the field of philosophy, freedom is a concept that is discussed widely and defined differently, usually with important consequences for other matters. Additionally, there is more than one kind of freedom humans can be said to possess. Freedom of the *will* refers to a person's ability to *act* in a way that is uncoerced, while freedom of the *intellect*, sometimes called *epistemic freedom*, refers to a person's ability to *think* or *believe* in a way that is uncoerced.

Swinburne's comment about too much evidence relates to both kinds of freedom. Some Christian philosophers and theologians have strongly emphasized the point that God is committed to ensuring we are genuinely free as we make the choice of whether to believe in him. In order to guarantee this freedom to believe, he sees to it that people who do not want to believe in him are not forced to do so by overpowering evidence. In other words, he will not overwhelm us with so much evidence that we cannot rationally reject belief in him even if we are looking for a way to do just that. Instead he guards both our *intellectual* freedom and our freedom of the *will* by providing evidence sufficient to direct people to him while, at the same time, allowing a person who *desires* to reject God to do so rationally. To do otherwise would constitute divine coercion of both the will and the intellect. As philosophers put it somewhat more technically, it would constitute epistemic obligation or force that could override a person's will and, because God is serious about guaranteeing our freedom in choosing or rejecting him, he will see to it that such epistemic coercion does not exist.

The seventeenth-century Christian Blaise Pascal is one of the philosophers who are helpful to reference for this discussion. Pascal was an outstanding individual by any standard. In addition to leaving a deep imprint on the world of religion, he was a brilliant mathematician known especially for his work on probability theory. He was also a scientist of proven ability who worked on barometric pressure and a technologist capable of designing and constructing a calculating machine. Furthermore, he devised and saw inaugurated the first public transit service in Paris. These achievements put him in the top rank of European intellectuals in his day. Even Sam Harris recognizes Pascal's genius, commenting on his "nimble mind."[24]

More importantly for our discussion, Pascal's accomplishments show he was a person who understood and appreciated evidence. If anyone knew both its benefits and limitations, it was Pascal, and his comments on the nature of the evidence for God are particularly fascinating. Long before Dawkins, Pascal declared that had God wished to provide overwhelming evidence for his own existence such that no one, including the most ardent atheist, could rationally refuse to believe in him, he could have done so. Indeed, it would have been easy. In Pascal's words,

> If he had wished to overcome the obstinacy of the most hardened, he could have done so by revealing himself to them so plainly that they could not doubt the truth of his essence. . . . [God] wished to make himself perfectly recognizable . . . to appear openly to those who seek him with all their heart and [hide himself] from those who shun him . . . by giving signs which can be seen by those who seek him and not by those who do not. There is enough light for those who desire only to see, and enough darkness for those of a contrary disposition.[25]

In other words, God refuses to overwhelm people with evidence for himself even though he could easily do it. Instead, he reveals himself plainly to those who sincerely seek him but not to those who do not. Pascal recognizes the obvious fact that there are people who choose (i.e., by an act of their will) not to believe in God. They do not *want* to believe and would rather there be no God. Pascal's contention is that God will give them exactly what they desire, namely the opportunity to *not* believe in him. He will not overwhelm them with evidence forcing their *mind* to accept his existence when their *will* has chosen not to believe, even though he could easily do so. The contemporary atheist philosopher Thomas Nagel is a good example of such a nonbeliever, as seen in his astonishingly honest words:

> I speak from experience, being strongly subject to this fear [of religion] myself; some of the most intelligent and well-informed people I know are religious believers. It isn't just that I don't believe in God and, naturally, hope that I'm right in my belief. It's that I hope there is no God! *I don't want there to be a God*; I don't want a universe to be like that.[26]

Nagel does not want to believe, and Pascal's contention is that God will see to it that the amount of evidence is such that he, and others like him, will be able to find rational ways of not believing in God. If God overwhelmed people like this with evidence for himself, says Pascal, he would be forcing an intellectual assent to his existence *against their will*, and that is something he will not do. He guarantees that those who believe in him and enter into a relationship with him do so *freely*.

We may wonder why God does it this way. We may even think he should have done things differently. But Pascal offers a reason for thinking God acted wisely in this matter. He explains it this way: "God wishes to move the *will* rather than the *mind*. Perfect clarity would help the mind and harm the will."[27]

This is a rather profound idea that finds agreement today in popular culture as seen in the well-known, popular expression, "A person convinced against his will is of the same opinion still." The idea is that if God provided evidence of himself that is convincing even to people who wish to reject him, it would clarify matters for their *minds* but in the process run roughshod over their *will* that still desires to reject God. This is something God will not do, and in a real sense, he is no different from any of us in this regard. Who among us would force relationships on people who deep down wish they could avoid the whole thing but for some reason cannot? It wouldn't be much of a relationship, would it? Once we see that God, too, is a person, albeit a divine person, who desires real relationships with other persons, this action on his part becomes perfectly intelligible.

Against this background, Swinburne's carefully made statement, "There is quite a lot of evidence . . . of God's existence, and too much might not be good for us,"[28] is nothing more than a recognition that perhaps a God who created humans to have eternal relationships with him might have a good reason for providing "a lot of evidence" but not so much as to overwhelm us since to do so would force people to believe in him intellectually, thus destroying their freedom. There is nothing absurd about this statement, and it certainly does not devalue evidence. If anything, it recognizes the importance of evidence and why God treats it with such great care in his desire to woo us rather than force himself upon us.

Dawkins Is Self-Refuting

We should not end this section without drawing attention to a contradiction in Dawkins's approach to arguing that Christianity is devoid of evidence for its truth claims. While he makes this claim repeatedly, he has also critiqued a number of arguments for the existence of God put forward by Aquinas. But if there is no evidence or argument for Christian truth claims, such as the existence of God, then why critique it? The fact that he critiques evidence is hard to square with his repeated assertion that there is no evidence.[29]

Nor is this a minor point. Dawkins has claimed all along that the nonevidential character of religion is what causes religious people to believe irrational ideas that, in turn, lead some of them to commit violent acts. It is the nonevidential nature of religion that is at the heart of religion's worst defect. Worse yet, there is no chance of reasoning with religious people concerning their beliefs precisely because they are not based on evidence. But why, then, does Dawkins attempt to refute the very evidence he claims does not exist?

One might suppose he actually means Christianity has no *good* evidence. That is what most of us might mean by making such a claim. If that were his intention, it would be a more reasonable claim, although one that would be notoriously difficult to support since doing so would require a careful analysis and rebuttal of all the evidence ever brought forward in defense of Christianity's truth claims. Dawkins has not even attempted such an enormous project, and in any case, this is almost surely not what he means given the overall picture he paints of Christianity.

He does not describe it simply as a belief system resting on evidence that happens to be weak. Rather, he goes to great lengths to argue that unlike his own field of science, Christianity, by its nature, has no concern for evidence whatsoever. Its claims are based on faith in holy books and holy men since that is how religions work. Evidence is simply not relevant to how truth claims are derived or believed.

As we have seen, this is a misrepresentation of Christianity, and Dawkins now seems to admit this, however implicitly. The fact that he responds to arguments for Christian belief put forward by Christian thinkers is an unspoken admission that they do have a concern for evidence and for justifying their beliefs after all. His own agreement or disagreement with this evidence is hardly the issue here. The point is that by replying to it, he admits it exists and that Christianity is not devoid of evidence for its truth claims.

The new critics of religion do not stop here, however. As we noted earlier in this book, a number of them portray religion, particularly Christianity, as intrinsically opposed to science. So it is time to ask if this claim is true.

5

Is Christianity Anti-Scientific?

Are the ways of religion contrary to the methods of science? Do members of the scientific community find themselves locked in a perpetual struggle against the opposing forces of religion as they examine evidence and pursue new and exciting knowledge of our universe? Many of the new critics of religion certainly think so, and it is worth quoting again the passage from Dawkins's book *The God Delusion* to see why. Religious people who read and believe their Scriptures, he says,

> know they are right because they have read the truth in a holy book and they know, in advance, that nothing will budge them from their belief. . . . The book is true, and if the evidence seems to contradict it, it is the evidence that must be thrown out, not the book.

Conversely, Dawkins states:

> I, as a scientist, believe . . . not because of reading a holy book but because I have studied the evidence. It really is a very different matter. . . . As a scientist, I am hostile to fundamentalist religion because it actively debauches the scientific enterprise. It teaches us not to change our minds, and not to want to know exciting things that are available to be known.[1]

93

Sam Harris agrees and describes science as the discipline that "represents our most committed effort to verify that our statements about the world are true (or at least not false)." It operates "by observation and experiment within the context of a theory."[2] On the contrary, he says that religious people believe what they do because God wrote their beliefs in a book, their particular Scriptures. This, he says, puts religious beliefs "beyond the scope of rational discourse." They "float entirely free of reason and evidence," and "most religions offer no valid mechanism by which their core beliefs can be tested and revised." As we saw earlier, this leads him to define religious faith as "simply unjustified belief in matters of ultimate concern . . . belief, in the absence of evidence."[3]

It is time for us to ask if it is really true that religion stands as a persistent enemy of the entire scientific enterprise. In other words, if we take our religious faith seriously and believe in the authority of our Scriptures, will we of necessity be at odds with science? If so, it really does mean that in order for science to make any headway at all it must continually resist religious forces or, even better, do away with religion altogether. There are at least three responses one can make to this charge.

Worldviews and Live Options

The first response is that, interestingly, there is a technical sense in which Dawkins is correct. People with religious convictions, like all other people, operate within certain frameworks of belief or worldviews. A worldview consists of the set of basic assumptions a person holds, whether consciously or subconsciously, about the origin and nature of the world, humans, other living beings, morals, values, and where we are all going.[4] Worldviews give meaning to our lives, they guide us in how to interpret our surroundings, and most importantly for our discussion, they exclude certain ideas from the realm of live options we are willing to consider. For example, most of us living in the Western world would not even consider the possibility that something we have lost, such as a wallet or set of keys, has simply disappeared into thin air. This just does not strike us as a viable suggestion, and we will not waste a moment of our time thinking about it. The lost item may have dropped out of our pocket, been stolen, or been misplaced, but to think it has just disappeared into thin air is not even worth discussing. Our response to anyone who might suggest otherwise will be something along the lines of: "Surely you can't be serious!" Furthermore, we will continue to hold this view even when all other explanations we can think of have been exhausted. After looking everywhere for the lost item, we will probably say something like, "Well, I don't know what happened to it, but I know it didn't just disappear into thin air."

A religious worldview, likewise, will exclude certain ideas from consideration. A Christian will find it difficult, if not impossible, to accept the notions that miracles are impossible or that there is no God, since such ideas are incompatible with the most basic assumptions of a Christian worldview. To this degree, Dawkins is correct.

He seems to be unaware, however, that this fact is true for all worldviews—including his own atheistic naturalism. He writes as though he is open to following evidence wherever it leads with no restrictions whatsoever on the conclusions he is willing to adopt, but of course this is not true. Naturalism, by definition, rules out in advance the possibility of anything miraculous or supernatural. Therefore, regardless of the data, a naturalist worldview will never allow conclusions that permit even consideration of the supernatural as a live option. Naturalists have no choice but to reject such conclusions.

In other words, the limiting and excluding functions of worldviews apply to Dawkins in the same way they apply to people with religious views. If religious people are victims of their worldviews, then Dawkins is no less a victim of his own.

What this means is that Dawkins's statement, quoted above, could be turned on its head and reflected back to Dawkins himself. For instance, when it comes to evidence pointing toward a divine origin of the universe or the occurrence of a miracle such as the bodily resurrection of Jesus from the dead, Dawkins has determined in advance that this did not occur because, as a naturalist, he "knows" miracles do not happen. Nothing will budge him from his belief, and if the evidence seems to contradict it, it is the evidence that must be thrown out or reassessed, not the conclusion. The only possible way he could accept something that does not fit his atheistic naturalism is to change his worldview and adopt a new one that does allow for the supernatural or miraculous. And of course, that option is also open to the religious person to consider the atheistic naturalist worldview.

Charles Templeton and Antony Flew stand out as well-known examples of people who, after prolonged thinking, changed their worldview stances. Templeton moved from Christian theism to what he calls reverent agnosticism, while Flew moved from atheism to theism. It was possible for these changes to occur because these men were willing to consider other worldviews as valid. But as long as a person operates within his or her own worldview—and everyone operates within one—he or she will exclude certain ideas because of that worldview. And this fact is as true of Dawkins's worldview as it is of anyone else's.

In fact, as incredible as it may sound to Dawkins and others, naturalism in certain cases is *more* limiting than the worldviews of many Christians since it rules out all explanations involving either a divine Creator or anything supernatural, including miracles. G. K. Chesterton, writing in 1908, found it amusing that the naturalist viewpoint is usually thought of as the liberal, free-thinking philosophy when, in reality, it is far more restrictive than views that allow for the possibility of miracles. He mused that "for some extraordinary reason, there is a fixed notion that it is more liberal to disbelieve in miracles than to believe in them. Why, I cannot imagine, nor can anybody tell me." He asks why the naturalist always has disbelieved the report of any miracle. Not because his viewpoint *allowed* him to deny it; rather, he "disbelieved miracles because his very strict materialism did *not allow* him to believe it."[5]

Chesterton's point is well taken. The atheistic naturalist is not free even to consider the option that an intelligent Creator stands behind the universe regardless of where the evidence points. He simply cannot go there; it is not a live option since his worldview rules out the notion of a Creator. Many Christians, on the other hand, while being open to the possibility of miracles and an intelligent cause of the universe, are also open to natural explanations for things if the evidence leads there, so long as God is considered the ultimate cause of everything.

It looks, then, as if Christians are in no worse shape, and in some cases are in a better position, than the new atheists when it comes to exploring ideas and following evidence. The upshot of it all is that there is no reason to think Christians are prevented from engaging in good science by their worldviews any more than Dawkins or Harris are by theirs.

But perhaps we should ask what really takes place in the world of science. Do we find people with religious faith, particularly Christians, engaging in science? Or is Dawkins right in asserting that in the real world religion and religious people "actively debauch the scientific enterprise"? Do religious faith and, more specifically, belief in the authority of Scripture cause us "not to want to know exciting things that are available to be known,"[6] as he puts it? Do they somehow put one at odds with the scientific enterprise?

The Illusion of Conflict

The reality is that nothing could be further from the truth. Many in the scientific community understand full well that there is no inherent conflict between religion and science and, in fact, many of the founders of modern science believed in God. These include Isaac Newton and Robert Boyle, who wrote extensively on theology as well as science; and Johannes Kepler and Jan Baptist van Helmont, who included many prayers and theological musings in their scientific notebooks. Even atheist Stephen Jay Gould, who was America's leading evolutionary biologist and Harvard professor until his death in 2002, makes it clear in his book *Rock of Ages* that the natural sciences are entirely consistent with religious belief, and thus, one does not have to give up religious belief in order to be an honest scientist. He observes that many of his evolutionary biologist colleagues were religious believers, and he says this about them: "Either half my colleagues are enormously stupid, or else the science of Darwinism is fully compatible with conventional religious beliefs—and equally compatible with atheism."[7]

Dawkins is bewildered by this notion coming, as it does, from such a noted scientist, and after considering its full import, he finally says, "I simply do not believe that Gould could possibly have meant much of what he wrote in *Rock of Ages*."[8] That is hardly a refutation. Not only did Gould mean what he said, just as Dawkins means what he says, but professional scientists have remained about as religious as almost everyone else in the general population and far more so than their academic colleagues in the arts and social sciences, a detail attested to by American science historian Rodney Stark.[9]

In other words, despite Dawkins's and Harris's assertions of an inherent conflict between religion and science, such a conflict simply does not exist, and the reason is clear. As the vast majority of Christians well know, the Bible was never intended to be read as a science textbook and, obviously, most Christians in the science community do not read it as one. The Bible is a revelation from God in which he tells us important things about himself, about ourselves, about how to live well, and most importantly, about God's loving plan to reconcile the human race to himself. When it comes to scientific knowledge, the Bible declares to us that God created the world, but it spends very little time telling us how he did it—only a few chapters in the beginning of a very large book. While Christians hold differing interpretations on these early chapters, most happily recognize that discovering the details of how God created the world and how it operates is the work of scientists.

Even St. Augustine (AD 354–430), Christianity's greatest theologian between Paul and Aquinas, makes it clear that biblical texts that deal with the origins of the world are not intended to be so rigidly interpreted that they leave no room for information from other sources that may bear upon the question at hand. In his words, "We should not rush in headlong and so firmly take our stand on one side that, if further progress in the search of truth justly undermines this position, we too fall with it. That would be to battle not for the teaching of Holy Scripture but for our own."[10]

He presses his point further by calling on Christians to refrain from making absurd statements about the teaching of the Bible when such statements flatly contradict what people already know from other reliable sources.[11] It is an error, he says, to dogmatically commit Scripture to certain interpretations that can easily be shown to be false by other disciplines of study. His words to this effect bear reading:

> A non-Christian knows something about the earth, the heavens, and the other elements of this world, about the motion and orbit of the stars and even their size and relative positions, about the predictable eclipses of the sun and moon, the cycles of the years and seasons, about the kinds of animals, shrubs, stones, and so forth, and this knowledge he holds to as being certain from reason and experience. Now, it is a disgraceful and dangerous thing for . . . [a non-Christian] to hear a Christian, presumably giving the meaning of Holy Scripture, talking nonsense on these topics. . . . The shame is not so much that an ignorant individual is derided, but that people outside the household of the faith think our sacred writers held such opinions.[12]

St. Augustine's advice has been taken by many, and when it is, there is no inherent conflict between religion and science. Furthermore, many scientists have operated and continue to operate within a Christian framework of thought, their scientific efforts being inspired and motivated by their Christian convictions. Just as one's admiration for the builder of a complex machine grows as one better understands the inner workings of the machine, in the same way, many Christians working in the field of science find that their sense of awe concerning the Creator of the world grows as they understand more of the complexity and wonder of his creation. Incredibly, this means the Christian worldview, rather than detracting from the scientific enterprise, actually encourages it.

David Shotton, lecturer in cell biology in the department of zoology at Oxford University, describes *The Soul of Science* as a magnificent book that "should be required reading for . . . all practicing scientists." In this book, Harvard chemist Charles Thaxton and science writer Nancy Pearcey state that whereas the image of the relationship between science and religion most of us grew up with was one of conflict and hostility,

> this conception is actually a *mis*conception, and one of recent lineage. Over some three centuries, the relationship between faith and science can best be described as an alliance. The scientist living between 1500 and 1800 inhabited a very different universe from that of the scientist living today. The earlier scientist was very likely to be a believer who did not think scientific inquiry and religious devotion incompatible. On the contrary, his motivation for studying the wonders of nature was a religious impulse to glorify the God who had created them.[13]

Colin Russell, professor of history of science, technology, and medicine at the Open University in the United Kingdom and an affiliated research scholar at Cambridge University, agrees in his book *Cross-Currents: Interactions between Science and Faith* that the idea of a war between science and religion is a relatively recent invention. He points to nineteenth-century thinkers such as Thomas Henry Huxley (1825–1895), John William Draper (1811–1882), and Andrew Dickson White (1832–1918) who, he says, carefully nurtured this conception of conflict out of a desire to overthrow the cultural dominance of Christianity, particularly the Anglican Church. Whatever one thinks of this depiction of their motives, many of their conclusions were rejected by significant philosophers and historians such as Alfred North Whitehead and Michael B. Foster, who around the same time argued that far from impeding the progress of science, Christianity had actually provided the soil in which it could flourish. The Christian culture within which science arose, they said, did not threaten science but actually helped to birth it. This leads to our third response—one that no doubt will come as a surprise to many.

Christianity's Surprising Contribution to Science

Not only is there no inherent conflict between science and religion, but as incredible as it may sound, many in the world of science have gone further by contending that the scientific enterprise as we know it would probably not exist had it not been for Christianity. They have had plenty of reasons for making this contention. After immersing himself in recent science historical studies, Rodney Stark asserts that while most people in Western culture will be surprised by this notion, it has "already become the conventional wisdom among historians of science."[14] In fact, it is so widely accepted among this group that Stark considered omitting from his book the chapter in which he argues this case, which deals with the history of science, because it seemed redundant and unnecessary. In the end he decided to include it for the sake of the wider public.

In what sense does the scientific enterprise owe its existence to Christianity? Stark's answer, in a nutshell, is that Christianity's view of the world and universe was essential for the rise of science and that without it science would, in all probability, never have arisen. In his words, "Christianity depicted God as a rational, responsive, dependable, and omnipotent being and the universe as his personal creation, thus having a rational, lawful, stable structure, awaiting human comprehension."[15]

Nobel Prize–winning biochemist Melvin Calvin also recognized the foundational conviction among scientists that the universe is ordered, and he thought deeply about the source of this conviction. He reminisced about his own personal reflections on this subject in his book *Chemical Evolution*:

> As I try to discern the origin of that conviction, I seem to find it in a basic notion discovered 2000 or 3000 years ago, and enunciated first in the Western world by the ancient Hebrews: namely, that the universe is governed by a single God, and is not the product of the whims of many gods, each governing his own province according to his own laws. This monotheistic view seems to be the historical foundation for modern science.[16]

Earlier still, the eminent philosopher and mathematician Alfred North Whitehead, who coauthored *Principia Mathematica* with Bertrand Russell, shocked his Western audience during one of his Lowell Lectures at Harvard in 1925 by stating that science arose in Europe because of the widespread "faith in the possibility of science . . . derivative from medieval theology."[17] How could he make such a claim? Did he not know that religion is the mortal enemy of scientific enquiry as Dawkins, Harris, and others imply? On the contrary, Whitehead understood that while admittedly some Christians throughout history have opposed certain scientific explanations or breakthroughs, a Christian concept of God as conscious Creator, which had been impressed upon the medieval mind-set, not only created an openness to science but was *essential* for the rise of science. He explains his position this way:

> I do not think, however, that I have even yet brought out the greatest contribution of medievalism to the formation of the scientific movement. I mean the inexpugnable belief that every detailed occurrence can be correlated with its antecedents in a perfectly definite manner, exemplifying general principles.
>
> Without this belief the incredible labours of scientists would be without hope. It is this instinctive conviction, vividly posed before the imagination, which is the motive power of research—that there is a secret, a secret which can be unveiled. How has the conviction been so vividly implanted in the European mind?
>
> When we compare this tone of thought in Europe with the attitude of other civilizations when left to themselves, there seems but one source of its origin. It must come from the medieval insistence on the rationality of God, conceived as with the personal energy of Jehovah and with the rationality of a Greek philosopher. Every detail was supervised and ordered. . . . Remember I am not talking about the explicit beliefs of a few individuals. What I mean is the impress on the European mind arising from the unquestioned faith of centuries. By this I mean the instinctive tone of thought and not a mere creed of words.[18]

Whitehead goes on to argue that the conceptions of God found in non-Christian religions and worldviews are simply too impersonal or irrational to sustain science. In these understandings of God, any particular event might be the result of an irrational, tyrannical God or be produced by some impersonal, inscrutable origin of things. This does not produce the level of confidence that one can understand the world that comes from belief in the intelligible rationality of a personal Creator.

Whitehead's analysis is insightful. Pagan religions tend to be animistic or pantheistic according to whether the natural world is regarded as either the dwelling place of the divine or an emanation of God's own essence. The most well-known form of animism holds that spirits or gods reside in nature; rocks and streams are alive with spirits and demons.[19] In other systems of non-Christian thought, there is no creation at all. The universe is believed to be eternal; it may go through an infinite number of cycles, but it has no purpose and, of course, no creator. Consequently, the universe is thought to be a supreme mystery, inconsistent, unpredictable, and arbitrary. Again, this provides no confidence that one can understand the world and therefore no impetus for the development of scientific study. The path to wisdom is through meditation and mystical insights.

Biblical teaching on creation is radically different. The planets are not divine, and God is not the world's soul. Rather he is its Creator. It is the product of his workmanship, as a table is the product of a carpenter's labor. Whitehead's point is that a particular conception of a Creator of the universe, and thus of the universe itself, was necessary for the rise of science, and Judeo-Christianity provided these conceptions.

The point here is that science developed out of a Christian worldview because people shaped by this context *believed it could be done*. God's creation can be studied and learned, and the more we understand it, the more deeply we will appreciate both it and its Creator. In Starks's words,

> Centuries of meditation will produce no empirical knowledge, let alone science. But to the extent that religion inspires efforts to comprehend God's handiwork, knowledge will be forthcoming, and science arises. . . . And that's precisely how not only the Scholastic scientists but also those who took part in the great achievements of the sixteenth and seventeenth centuries saw themselves—as in the pursuit of the secrets of the Creation.[20]

One question remains, however: Didn't other early non-Christian civilizations also have science? After all, cultures such as the Chinese, Greeks, and Romans had organized knowledge, academies for learning, and even technology. Can we be so sure that science arose only in Western European civilization?

This is a question others have addressed more fully than we can here, and the interested reader is well advised to pursue it further.[21] But a few comments on Chinese civilization are in order since the Chinese are well known for their early technology and cultural progress. While one might think such a culture would also have developed science, the Chinese did not do so.

Bertrand Russell wrote of the lack of science in early Chinese culture and was baffled by it. Given their cultural progress, one would think the Chinese might have developed science long before Europe. In his book *The Problem of China*, he wrote that "although Chinese culture has hitherto been deficient in science it never contained anything hostile to science, and therefore the spread of scientific knowledge encounters no such obstacles as the Church put in its way in Europe."[22]

Russell expected that the growth of Chinese science would have far surpassed Western science. What went wrong? It appears he failed to notice what Whitehead saw, that the concept of a conscious Creator, which gave birth to science in the West, was virtually absent from Chinese culture, and for this reason science didn't grow as it did in the West.

Marxist historian Joseph Needham, who devoted most of his career and many volumes to the history of Chinese technology, drew precisely this conclusion. After searching for a nonreligious, materialist explanation for the failure of the early Chinese to develop science, he finally concluded that the Chinese simply had no belief in a rational, personal Creator who had ordered the universe such that it would function according to rational laws and could be comprehended in physical terms. In Needham's words,

> The conception of a divine celestial lawgiver imposing ordinances on non-human nature never developed. . . . It was not that there was no order in Nature for the Chinese, but rather that it was not an order ordained by a rational personal being, and hence there was no conviction that rational personal beings would be able to spell out in their lesser earthly languages the divine code of laws which he had decreed aforetime. The Taoists, indeed, would have scorned such an idea as being too naïve for the subtlety and complexity of the universe as they intuited it.[23]

Perhaps a cautionary note is in order here. If we are correct in believing that a particular conception of the world was *necessary* for the rise of science, we should not make the mistake of thinking it is or ever was *sufficient* as a cause. Many other cultural and social developments were also necessary to facilitate both the origin and the spread of science. These include the growth of trade and commerce, technological advances, scientific institutions, and the circulation of journals. In other words, if a Stone Age culture suddenly converted to Christianity en masse, we would still not expect them to develop science anytime soon. And this is precisely the point: There are some societies in which one would have expected to see science arise, but it did not because these societies lacked something essential to its rise. In the case of the Chinese, they lacked certain key assumptions about the world and its origins.

6

Is Biblical Morality Appalling?

We saw in chapter 1 that the new critics of religion are bewildered and angered by the morality they see taught in the Bible, and few have expressed this anger more vehemently than Richard Dawkins. When he looks in the Bible, he finds misogyny, vindictiveness to enemies, penalties far harsher than they ought to be for the crimes committed—including some for actions that ought not to be penalized at all, such as acting on one's personal sexual preferences—and far more. In the end, as we noted earlier, he describes the God of the Old Testament as "arguably the most unpleasant character in all fiction: jealous and proud of it; a petty, unjust, unforgiving control-freak; . . . homophobic, racist, infanticidal, genocidal, . . ." and on it goes.[1] The Jesus of the New Testament was better but only insofar as he was not content to derive his ethics from the Old Testament.

What are we to make of this picture of biblical morality and the God behind it? The first thing to remember is that all texts must be interpreted within their historical, social, and literary contexts. This is especially true of texts that seem puzzling to us due to the great historical and cultural distances that separate us from them. To do otherwise is to impose on a text present-day standards that are not relevant to the time the text was written; it is to misread the texts. That is one reason all of us must be especially cautious in making bold and condemnatory statements about the meaning of texts that were written in times and places far removed from our own.

Dawkins has not taken such care when interpreting biblical texts, and it undermines his attack on the morality he finds there. As Alister McGrath points out, Dawkins's strongly negative attitude toward the Bible as a whole is based on a superficial engagement with its core themes, an inadequate knowledge of the biblical text itself, and a highly selective treatment of certain passages.[2] In *The God Delusion* he expresses great indignation at the Hebrew Scriptures, but all except two of his quotations are from the first five books of the Bible; the other two are from the book of Judges, and none whatsoever are taken from the other thirty-three books of the Old Testament. Can anyone claim to be fairly representing the teachings of a book as large and diverse as the Old Testament when their material is exclusively drawn from a select few places in it?

Calling Paul the author of the New Testament book of Hebrews[3] is a give-away mistake that would typically be made by a first-year theology student. He or she would soon discover that while the author of this book is unknown, the majority opinion for a few centuries has been that it is not Paul, and therefore the standard way of referring to the author is simply, "the author of Hebrews." It is the type of error that shows Dawkins's knowledge of the text he so adamantly ridicules is very superficial indeed.

He also seems oblivious to the common distinction in all literature between actions that are *prescribed* and those that are merely *described*. At times it even appears that as far as he is concerned, any action reported in the pages of Scripture is thereby approved and justified by it. Consider the way he uses certain stories in the Old Testament in his contorted attempts to prove it is a misogynistic book. One such story is of a group of men in the city of Gibeah who gang-rape a young woman until she dies. In the morning, the man she had been traveling with responds by carving her body into pieces and sending them out as a summons to war (Judg. 19:1–29).[4]

It is a horrific story, but Dawkins's use of it to try to show a misogynistic attitude in the Bible could not be more misguided, as an examination of the larger context shows. Judges, the book containing this story, states from beginning to end that this was a time when every person turned away from following God and did "what was right in his own eyes" (Judg. 17:6; 21:25; see also Judg. 2:11–12; 4:1; 6:1; 10:6; 13:1), and the results were often appalling. In other words, this book is not God's *prescription* of how to act but rather a *description* of what happens when people reject his prescriptions. No one would blame a physician for the death of a diabetic patient who rejected the doctor's instructions and followed a diet of cola and candy instead. Nor would anyone reading a report of such an incident take it as an endorsement of a cola and candy diet.

Perhaps the most head-shaking part of Dawkins's attempt to show that the God of the Bible is a misogynist is the way he compares the story of Jephthah, the Israeli general who sacrifices his daughter after making a woefully tragic promise (Judg. 11:30–39), with the story in Genesis 22, when God intervenes to stop Abraham from sacrificing his son Isaac. Dawkins compares these two stories and argues that when it is the life of a young boy at stake, Isaac, God sees fit to intervene to save his life, but in the case of a girl, Jephthah's daughter, God cannot be bothered to step in. The misogyny is patent, Dawkins declares.[5]

But the comparison is entirely arbitrary, and God's reasons for acting as he did in these two stories have nothing to do with the genders of the people involved. In the case of Jephthah, we have the normal case of a person making an utterly dreadful promise—one he ought never to have made—to sacrifice the first person to come out of his house upon his return home from battle if God will give him the victory. As happens in most cases then and now, God allows him to experience the consequences of his actions, as tragic as they are.

The story of Abraham and Isaac, however, is not a normal case of a person initiating and carrying out an action of his own accord. In this story, God orchestrates the entire event from beginning to end. He calls Abraham to take this action, gives him step-by-step instructions, and knows all along that he has no intention of ordering or allowing Abraham to kill his son, Isaac. Abraham follows God's instructions, and it is part of his personal preparation to be the founding father of the Jewish nation.

We may wish God would have prevented Jephthah from following through on his promise, but I'm not sure we know what we're wishing for. As C. S. Lewis has shown in his insightful book *The Problem of Pain*, our lives as free agents could hardly go on if God continually intervened to prevent the bad consequences of our actions, as people like Dawkins claim he would do if he existed.[6]

Suppose God did intervene; then where should he stop? Should he turn a baseball bat into a soft twig when it is being used to strike someone, a bad word into a good one when it is being spewed out to demean someone, or a harmful thought into a kind one as it is being formed? God could do all of these, but then we would be robots or something close to it. Jephthah merely functioned like a normal human being, making decisions and acting on them, and he experienced the consequences of his actions as we all do. These two stories have nothing to do with gender or with misogyny on God's part, and these conclusions can only be drawn if a person approaches the two stories looking for a way to read these themes into them.

Other misstatements by Dawkins concerning biblical teaching include his assertion that the doctrine of original sin "lies at the heart of New Testament theology."[7] It does no such thing. And in fact, that doctrine is a teaching developed by Augustine centuries after Jesus's time on earth. When we read the New Testament text carefully, we find that Jesus does not talk about sin very much. His baseline assumption, as expressed in John 3:16–18, is that the world is in need of redemption because of its sin, and his purpose in coming is "not to condemn the world, but that the world might be saved through him" (v. 17). His primary message is not sin but *redemption*. Even the apostle Paul, who does talk more about sin, especially in the first chapters of Romans, is primarily devoted to the notion of *forgiveness* for sins. Sin, he says, is the problem not just of a few people or groups here or there but of the whole world. "All have sinned," he says in Romans 3:23, and therefore all are in need of forgiveness, which was the primary message he desired to communicate everywhere he went.

Indeed, it sometimes looks as though Dawkins is not even concerned to do the work necessary to interpret the Bible properly, as is shown by his airy dismissal of the entire book of Revelation as "one of the weirdest books in the Bible."[8] Revelation is an example of the genre called *apocalyptic literature*, a genre that requires painstaking work and not a little humility on the part of its interpreters. Dawkins shows no interest in trying to understand this genre.

This is a troubling sign that shows Dawkins has no interest in seriously engaging the texts he finds so offensive to see whether real solutions might exist. Rather, it increasingly looks as though his aim is merely to launch a polemic against the Bible. The fact is that many thoughtful Christians have puzzled over some of these same Old Testament passages, and Christian theologians have seriously engaged them, giving due care to rules of interpretation and context.

A careful examination of the Old Testament reveals that the texts that make it up were developed among a group of people, the Israelites, who were continually at war with their neighbors. On the one hand they were fighting off the nations and tribes around them, while on the other hand they were trying desperately to establish and maintain their own identity as a group. This was no small struggle, but it did not end there. In the midst of it all, they were only gradually coming to learn about their God, one piece at a time as it were. Their Scriptures were given to them not as one completed whole but rather, through a process we now refer to as *progressive revelation*, God was revealed to them in their Scriptures over approximately a thousand years. Throughout that time, the people of Israel came to understand more and more about their God.

Even from their earliest history, however, we find alongside the passages Dawkins apparently finds so appalling other material of which he seems to have no knowledge. In the very books from which he quotes there are passages instructing the people of Israel to show compassion, kindness, and forgiveness toward others. In Deuteronomy, the fifth book of the Old Testament, the Israelites are called to show hospitality to strangers (Deut. 10:17–19), while the book of Leviticus sets strict limits on how far a person may go in exacting revenge from a person who has wronged him or her (Lev. 19:18). This same book also forbids slavery (Lev. 25:39–43) and infant sacrifice, a common practice by Israel's neighbors that Israel continually fell into (Lev. 18:21; 20:2). It even calls for a Year of Jubilee for debt to help the poorest and most vulnerable among them (Lev. 25:8–55, especially vv. 25–28). In all these instructions, from the very books Dawkins quotes, we gain a fuller and far more positive picture of biblical moral teaching and the God who is behind it than is represented by the one Dawkins paints in *The God Delusion*.

Things are even more interesting if we look to other parts of the Old Testament—parts that Dawkins has totally ignored, such as the Prophets and the wisdom literature. The story of Israel in the Old Testament is a story of a people who continually strayed in one way or another from God's highest purposes for them. Sometimes they exploited the weak and vulnerable, and other times they overemphasized cultic rituals at the expense of God's real requirements. In the Prophets we find God's spokespersons continually calling Israel back and, in doing so, revealing some of the greatest moral insights ever voiced by humans. The prophet Isaiah sternly proclaimed that Israel had placed so much emphasis on religious ceremonies and practices that she had not lived up to her more important duties to "seek justice, correct oppression, defend the fatherless, plead for the widow" (Isa. 1:17, see vv. 12–17). The prophet Micah similarly points out that due to the people's obsession with religious rituals such as burnt offerings and sacrifices, they have neglected God's real moral requirements, which are "to do justice, and to love kindness, and to walk humbly with your God" (Micah 6:8; see vv. 6–8).

It is the prophet Jonah, however, who provides us with what is perhaps the most striking example in the Old Testament of the virtually unlimited mercy and forgiveness God desires to shower on people and that he calls on his people to demonstrate as well. Whatever one thinks of the historical factuality of all parts of this story, the point of it is that the only "fault" God had, even in the eyes of his prophet Jonah, was that of being too forgiving and merciful to the Ninevites, who deserved anything but mercy.

Nineveh was the capital city of the Assyrian Empire, whose soldiers were known for their brutality toward men, women, children, and property. People who care to read the details of their military campaigns should be warned to brace themselves for some particularly gruesome accounts. Jonah knew all too well of their practices, as did most Israelites and people in many other nations as well. For God to promise forgiveness to this group of people if they simply repented of their actions was too much. Jonah would have none of it. Sure enough, when he finally did bring the message of forgiveness to the people of this city after doing everything possible to get out of the job, they turned from their evil and violence and were shown God's mercy (Jonah 3:5–10). Jonah was furious. "This is what I said would happen," he told God angrily. His actual words are worth reading. "I knew that you are a gracious and compassionate God, slow to anger and abounding in love, a God who relents from sending calamity" (Jonah 4:2 NIV). For this, he will forever be known as the world's most unhappy successful evangelist. It was the success that made him unhappy.

The unfolding picture of God that one sees from a more complete look at the Old Testament is far different from the distorted description portrayed by Dawkins. It is of a God who is more repulsed by immorality than humans are but who also exceeds humans' willingness to forgive the evil he so strongly abhors. Repeatedly the Old Testament summarizes God's character and modus operandi as "merciful and gracious, slow to anger and abounding in steadfast love" (Ps. 103:8; see also Ps. 145:8; Joel 2:13; Jonah 4:2–3).

What, then, are we to make of those perplexing actions and commands God gave that seem so harsh, such as the instructions to destroy certain groups of people or cities, including men, women, children, and animals? How do actions like these fit with the compassionate and forgiving character of God that we have seen set forth throughout the Old Testament?

In searching for an answer to this question, it is critically important to recognize that, as we noted earlier, if we are to understand the meaning of any specific actions, we must interpret them within the greater context in which they occur. In the case of these perplexing passages, the larger context is that God never intended Israel to be merely one *ordinary* nation among others. God had a special purpose for this nation that deeply influenced the way he dealt with them, and understanding this purpose sheds light on these puzzling passages. God intended for Israel to be a vehicle through which he could communicate his message of love and forgiveness to the people of the whole world. His plan was that by his interaction with Israel, people in other nations would come to know God and hear that he loves them and desires to show compassion and forgiveness to them. In the words of the book of Genesis, the first book of the Bible, the nation of Israel was intended to be a blessing to the nations (Gen. 12:1–3).

But anyone who has read the story of Israel in the Old Testament knows that it is a tragic story. The people are repeatedly enticed into the practices of the nations around them, including child sacrifice and idol worship, thereby perverting God's message to the nations. Even more relevant for us, however, is that it is also a story of God's willingness to take whatever steps necessary to see his purpose fulfilled through these continually wandering people so that the nations of the world could hear of his love for them.

The serious question, then, is whether God might have known that on certain occasions harsh actions—the kind we all puzzle over—were necessary in order for Israel to remain an effective vehicle for expressing and living out this message of Good News to the world. For example, could God have known that unless certain penalties were enacted—penalties Dawkins finds so unreasonable—the people of Israel would have been drawn into practices that would have made them ineffective as communicators of God's message of love and forgiveness to the world? After all, they certainly showed tendencies to wander.

To take another example, might God have known that unless a particularly violent and unjust civilization was destroyed, those re-

maining would simply grow up and reinstate the same practices that
would again entice Israel away? Jericho was a strategic city in the
Amalekite nation, which had attacked Israel repeatedly over the past
forty years (Exod. 17:8–14; Num. 21:1–3). Could it even be that unless
that city was destroyed, in an attack that Dawkins calls genocidal,
Israel would have been blocked in its attempt to establish a homeland
from which to communicate God's message of hope and love to the
surrounding nations?

It must be kept in focus that judgments like these came only after
God's repeated petitions to those cities to turn from their vicious ways
of living and a promise that God would relent from his judgment if
they did so.[9] To put this into today's context, we may ask how long
a person should be permitted to continue murdering, raping, or ter-
rorizing others before correction is brought—even harsh correction.
This promise from God to relent is stated explicitly by the prophet
Jeremiah:

> If at any time I announce that a nation or kingdom is to be uprooted,
> torn down and destroyed, and if that nation I warned repents of its
> evil, then I will relent and not inflict on it the disaster I had planned.
>
> Jeremiah 18:7–8 NIV

This principle is exemplified in the story of the city of Nineveh,
which heeded the words of Jonah, but it is also seen in the story of
Jericho. The people of this city saw Israel coming and even witnessed
them marching around their city six times over a period of six days.
They had ample time to reach out and heed the words of God through
this people if they wanted to. Instead they locked their doors, shut
their ears to anything God might have to say to them, and maintained
a hostile stance toward Israel. Even so, one citizen of Jericho named
Rahab chose to accept Israel's offer of peace, and just as Jeremiah had
promised, she was saved even while her city was not. It is a fascinating
story and demonstrates the lengths God was willing to go in order
to spare those who responded positively to him (Josh. 2:1–21; 6:17,
22–23). A few chapters later we find the nation of Gibeah also making
an offer of peace to Israel, and even though they employed deceptive
means to do so, they too were spared judgment (Josh. 9:3–20).

The picture that emerges is of a God who was never eager to hand
out judgment on anyone. He did so sadly and only as a last resort
to a nation or people who refused to turn from evil and accept his

forgiveness. The prophets of God describe him in precisely this way. Speaking through Ezekiel, God asks rhetorically,

> Do I take any pleasure in the death of the wicked? declares the Sovereign LORD. Rather, am I not pleased when they turn from their ways and live?
>
> Ezekiel 18:23 NIV

> Say to them, As I live, says the Lord GOD, I have no pleasure in the death of the wicked, but that the wicked turn from his way and live; turn back, turn back from your evil ways; for why will you die?[10]
>
> Ezekiel 33:11

It is a striking picture of God delighting when people turn from their destructive, evil ways and grieving over the judgment he feels compelled to send when they do not.

These are suggestions of some purposes God may have had for carrying out certain actions we find perplexing. Perhaps we think he should have had better reasons than these, and perhaps he does. Still, we may wonder what good reason could ever justify some of the things God did. Whatever merit these suggestions have, however, we must recognize that for us to pronounce any of God's actions in the Old Testament immoral or unjust requires that we somehow know beyond the shadow of a doubt that he did *not* have any good purposes whatsoever for taking the actions he did. But of course, none of us could possibly know this. It is, at the very least, *possible* that the God pictured in the Bible could have had morally sufficient reasons for his actions. To deny this, one would need to be omniscient.

A morally sufficient reason is one that removes blame from the person involved. It is the difference between a doctor inflicting pain on a child by giving her a medical injection and the school bully causing similar pain by holding the same child down and poking her with a needle. One is a good act while the other is cruel abuse, and the difference between the two is the presence of a morally sufficient reason in one case but not the other. All of us recognize this instinctively, whether we are trained philosophers or ordinary, thinking people who are called upon daily to make moral decisions.

Furthermore, the Old Testament is a story of God acting with purpose. He takes very intentional steps to execute a plan that involved using one nation of fallible human beings to communicate his love and forgiveness to other nations of equally fallible human beings. Considering this, it becomes not merely *possible* but highly *plausible* to believe God had good purposes even for the actions we find perplexing. His compassionate character and large purposes running through the entire Old Testament, which were for the benefit of the whole world, lend credence to the notion that this same love and compassion motivated even these puzzling actions in some way. After all, it was God's benevolent character that threw Jonah into a fit of anger.

To add another element, consider the fact that the child mentioned above has no knowledge of the doctor's reason for inflicting pain on her. All she sees is the doctor and her mother cooperating to cause her pain, and it's a miserable situation. The fact that she doesn't understand the good purpose behind this painful action does not, of course, mean there is no good purpose; indeed there is. The child's position is analogous to our own as we examine the Old Testament. We read of certain puzzling things God did, and we sometimes wonder what good reasons he could possibly have had for doing them. Again, our lack of knowledge on this point in no way proves he had no good purpose for these actions, especially given the fact that he is a God who acts with good purposes throughout the Old Testament.

Nor is this simply a convenient way out of a difficult problem. It is, in fact, a requirement for anyone wishing to prove God acted unjustly. When it comes to judging the morality of particular actions, it is one thing for us to know God carried out a particular action but an entirely different matter to know that this action, however puzzling or even troubling, is immoral or unjust. To know that, one would need to know that he carried it out without a good, morally sufficient reason. In one sense this is a rather obvious point that we all recognize on a day-to-day basis. Someone visiting North America from a foreign culture very different from our own may witness a man in a blue suit forcibly detain another man and place him behind bars in a large brick building down the street. Did the man in the blue suit act immorally and cruelly? It certainly appears that way to the visitor. But if the man in the uniform is a police officer arresting a criminal, we know otherwise. It all depends on the meaning of his actions, and to know that we must understand the context. Ultimately it depends on whether the man in the blue suit has a morally sufficient reason for his actions.

The power of a morally sufficient reason has been recognized widely and employed in other issues with great effect. For example, it has been influential in convincing many philosophers of religion that the traditional argument from evil against God is unsuccessful. This argument, in its most basic form, states that evil is logically incompatible with the existence of an all-powerful and completely good God, and since evil exists, God cannot exist. Alvin Plantinga, employing this reasoning, has argued convincingly that it is always possible that God could have a good reason for allowing some evil to exist in the world. Furthermore, from the fact that we may not know what that reason is, it does not follow that none exists. He presses the point further by asking the following question:

> Suppose that the theist admits he just doesn't know why God permits evil. What follows from that? Very little of interest. Why suppose that if God *does* have a good reason for permitting evil, the theist would be the first to know? Perhaps God has a good reason, but that reason is too complicated for us to understand. The fact that the theist doesn't know why God permits evil is, perhaps, an interesting fact about the theist, but by itself it shows little or nothing relevant to the rationality of belief in God.[11]

Applying this insight to the question at hand, it is possible that God has morally sufficient reasons for his actions in the Old Testament as well—even the puzzling ones—and the fact that we may not know with certainty what those reasons are hardly means none exist. As we have already seen, however, the case is even stronger when we take into account both the overarching character of God and the fact that throughout the Old Testament he acts with good purposes. For that reason it is not difficult to believe that he also had such purposes even for the actions we find perplexing. (We have suggested a few possible ones, and undoubtedly there are others.) All of this shows that it is not merely possible but highly plausible that even actions that are hard for us to comprehend are motivated by God's love and justice in some way.

This also shows why there is something absolutely odd about us finite and morally flawed people pointing the finger at an infinite God and claiming we know better than he what judgments are appropriate for which actions or that if we had been in his position, we would have done things differently. None of us can make such claims since we have neither the knowledge nor long-term perspective of an infinite God. What we can say is that the picture of God presented to us in the Old Testament is of a gracious and compassionate God who acts with good purposes for the benefit of the entire world.

Be that as it may, the biblical portrayal of God does not end with the Old Testament. A few hundred years after the final book of the Old Testament was written, Jesus of Nazareth appeared on the scene. And here an important point must be made. Dawkins complains that even though the Old Testament has a few "nice bits," they are strewn among the "nasty bits," and we are at a loss to decide which ones are the "moral bits" and which are not. By the "moral bits," he presumably means the ones we should follow. We need some criterion for this, he says, and Scripture provides none.

What he fails to understand is that Christians have provided precisely this criterion for two thousand years, namely the words and the example of Jesus of Nazareth, who claimed to have come for the very purpose of revealing God to us like never before. In other words, Jesus was the final and greatest revelation of God to the world. "He who has seen me has seen the Father," he told his disciples (John 14:9; see vv. 1–9). In the words of John's Gospel, Jesus, who was "in the bosom of the Father, . . . has made him known" (John 1:18). Interestingly, whereas Dawkins asserts that Jesus saw the Old Testament as a book in need of correction, Jesus claimed he had come to fulfill, not correct or disregard, the Jewish law (Matt. 5:17).

For this reason, Christians read and interpret the Old Testament Scriptures through a christological filter. The teachings and example of Jesus are the interpretive guide for understanding the Old Testament. This is why Christians have never attempted to put into practice the religious rituals of the Old Testament. Even more importantly for the question of religious violence—the focus of this book—Jesus did no violence to anyone. He was on the receiving end of plenty of violence, but he was never the source of it.

Furthermore, he understood the Old Testament principle well that all people have intrinsic dignity and value stemming from the fact that they are *all* purposeful creations of a loving God who made them in his own image (Gen. 1:26–27). But Jesus went further with this foundational principle; he showed what it means to live it out in the real world. It means:

giving to people in need when they ask for something (Matt. 5:40–42)

responding nonviolently to personal attacks by turning the other cheek (Matt. 5:39)

loving not just our friends but, incredibly, our enemies too (Matt. 5:43–44) forgiving others when they do wrong to us (Matt. 6:14–15)

avoiding hypocrisy of all kinds (Matt. 6:5–6, 16–18; 7:3–5)

At times Jesus was very specific in what it means to treat people with dignity. In his parable of the Good Samaritan, he taught his followers that they should be willing to change their schedules, if necessary, to provide care for people they came upon who were in great need, even if those people were members of a group with whom they did not normally associate (Luke 10:30–37). Actions like these, said Jesus, are in the character of God (Matt. 5:45).

Followers of Jesus today, therefore, rightly reject violence as a means to accomplishing their religious aims in this world. Of course, there are exceptions to this. Christians make mistakes; it is our willingness to learn from them that is critical. When on occasion certain people, claiming to be Christians, do resort to violence for religious reasons, their actions are condemned by the vast majority of followers of Jesus around the world, as they should be. Such actions fly in the face both of Jesus's example and of his explicit teaching.

This leads to a question: What have Jesus's followers done with his magnificent moral teachings? One would think that people who carry out teachings like these would be conspicuous in any crowd. One would also think the world would be a radically different place if even a small group of people lived this way. How could it possibly remain the same?

While Jesus's followers have, of course, always been fallible and imperfect people, many of them throughout the past two thousand years have been excited by his teachings and have taken steps to live them out, however imperfectly. And the world is indeed a different place because of them. Those who tried to pattern their lives after Jesus's moral teachings have brought about changes that improved the lives of many people of all ages, ethnicities, and social standings throughout the world. The story is an exciting one, and it shows not only that Christianity is *not* the root cause of the world's greatest evils—as some recent critics of religion contend—it is actually the source of many profound benefits for which we can all be grateful. It is to this remarkable and largely untold story that we now turn.

7

Living the Way Jesus Calls Us to Live

The misguided notion held by some critics of religion is that Christianity tends to produce people who are intolerant and prone to violence and who desire to impose their views on others. The reality is that the more authentic a person's commitment to Jesus's teachings, the more that person's entire way of thinking will promote values of human dignity and worth, equality, peace, and freedom of choice as well as a deep commitment to doing good deeds. These are values we can all appreciate. If practiced consistently by all people, the world would be a radically different place and there would be no need to write books dealing with the connection between religion and violence.

Unfortunately, as noted above, people who call themselves Christians have not always practiced Jesus's teachings. For example, at times they have enforced their views on others and shown a lack of tolerance toward people of other belief systems. Examples are found in the horrors that occurred during the Spanish Inquisition from 1478 to 1550, the church-sanctioned witch burnings in several countries about the same time, and the Act of Uniformity passed by England's Parliament in 1662, which established Anglicanism as the official religion in England and declared illegal any gathering of more than five people of any other faith.

These are sad episodes in Christian history and are rightly condemned by the vast majority of Christians today. What we must understand about them and the people behind them is that, in the words of Canadian political scientist John Redekop, "while these perpetrators of intolerance and brutality may have been true to the assertions of their particular religious groups, they were not true to the ethical teaching of Jesus, the Head of the church."[1] Furthermore, we ought not to judge biblical values and teachings by their neglect or abuse any more than we should judge atheism by the horrors inflicted by Stalin or Lenin. Most importantly, however, we should not allow these tragic episodes to overshadow the predominantly positive impact of biblical values in the world as they have been lived out by people around the globe.

Let us consider a few of the values mandated for followers of Jesus and then turn our attention to a number of specific achievements brought about by those who have practiced them.

Intrinsic Human Dignity

As we noted earlier, this is the foundational, ethical mandate for followers of Christ that underlies all the other moral teachings given by Jesus and shows why they make sense. Few teachings are more explicitly set forth in the Bible than that all human beings—regardless of race, belief, gender, social status, or geographical location—have intrinsic dignity and value stemming from the fact that they are purposeful creations of a loving God who made them "in his own image" (Gen. 1:27).

To say humans have intrinsic dignity or value is to say that their lives have value simply because they are human, not because of any other qualities they possess such as health, strength, or the ability to make a contribution to others. Furthermore, because this intrinsic dignity is due to the image of God in humans, it follows that *all* human beings have it. It is a small step from this idea to the conclusion that human beings are *equally* valuable in the eyes of their Creator.

Equality

The principle of human equality not only follows from the origin of human dignity as seen in the preceding section but also is taught explicitly in the Bible. While the notion of equality can be abused, as we have seen in this book, it is a powerful ideal with far-reaching implications for the treatment of our fellow human beings. The apostle Paul, in his letter to the Christians in Galatia, broke down all the common differences people of that day were using to create divisions and treat others better or worse: ethnicity, social status, and gender. He said that among followers of Christ "there is neither Jew nor Greek, there is neither slave nor free, there is neither male nor female; for you are all one in Christ Jesus" (Gal. 3:28). Because all people possess a spark of the divine, as it is sometimes called, all are of equal value and there is no hierarchy of worth or dignity. As the following pages will illustrate, where followers of Jesus have lived according to his teachings, differences and divisions have decreased and the principle of equality has gained wide acceptance.

When we think about it, it is difficult to overstate the importance of this principle for the way we treat people. When applied to society and government, it produces equality of rights as a basic starting point—equality before the law and equality in voting. It even extends to criminals, which means that incarcerated people must be treated fairly in law and humanely in prison. Even more significantly, it means that political leaders will be judged by the same standards as citizens because in spite of their current positions of power, they have no greater intrinsic dignity or worth than anyone else.

The Golden Rule

Jesus's instruction to his followers to "do to others what you would have them do to you" (Matt. 7:12 NIV) follows naturally from the intrinsic dignity of all human beings. After all, if others share the same value and worth as I do, it makes sense to treat them precisely as I want to be treated. This moral principle has come to be called the Golden Rule, and it is the perfect rule of thumb for our day-to-day interactions with others, which is what Jesus intended. His actual words were, "*In everything*, do to others what you would have them do to you, *for this sums up the Law and the Prophets*" (Matt. 7:12 NIV, italics mine). In other words, by following this one guiding moral principle in our dealings with others, we will find ourselves living in such a way that our other moral duties will tend to take care of themselves. If we follow this rule, we will not need to think much about the other principles. After all, who among us wants be stolen from, have harm brought to us, or be refused help when in need?

The power of this rule lies in its simplicity and ease of application. It has the almost uncanny ability to bring instant moral clarity to many confusing moral dilemmas we each face in our day-to-day dealings with others. By calling us to put the shoe on the other foot and ask ourselves how we would want to be treated if the situation were reversed, it often makes our moral duty instantly clear.

It is worth noting that Christianity does not lay out a detailed plan for how the Golden Rule is to be applied in particular situations. It was never intended to do this since such a plan would be impossible to construct. Any specific application plan that is suited to one situation would not suit another. This principle functions as a guiding principle and, just as in every field of study or work, the practitioners in each field need to take the initiative to figure out how it applies in specific cases.

The Golden Rule is perhaps the most widely known moral principle in the world. It sums up what virtually everyone already knows to be right. This highlights an important fact about Christ's moral teaching, namely that it contained very little that was really new. As C. S. Lewis was fond of saying, really great moral teachers never introduce new moralities; it is quacks and cranks who do that. The real job of great moral teachers is to keep bringing us back to the same old moral ideas we are all tempted to neglect, like a piano teacher brings a young student back to that part of the song she struggles with and wants to skip over.[2]

This raises the interesting question of what, precisely, Christianity has contributed in the realm of moral teaching. Clearly Jesus did not invent brand-new moral teachings, nor were he and his followers the only ones to teach the principles he set out. Confucius taught a similar version of the Golden Rule some five hundred years before Jesus's time.

Jesus's contribution consisted of developing moral ideas that were not technically new and extending them further, precisely as he did in the case of the Golden Rule. Whereas Confucius stated this rule negatively, "Do *not* do to others as you would *not* have them do to you,"[3] Jesus put it in positive terms: "*Do* to others as you would have them *do* to you" (Luke 6:31 NIV, italics mine). Rather than focus on all the things we should not do, he was far more concerned about what we should do. This is not a new or different rule than the one Confucius set out; rather, it is an extension or further development of it. C. S. Lewis noted that no one who disagreed with Confucius's version would have any reason to accept Jesus's Golden Rule. On the other hand, anyone who agreed with Confucius's version would immediately recognize Jesus's version as an extension or advance of the same rule.[4] Jesus's version reaches further and covers many more of our activities. This, of course, makes it a harder rule to live by but also one that, if carried out, will make a greater difference in the world.

Jesus did the same with other moral teachings, as can be seen in his treatment of the black-and-white rule against murder—a rule that was well known in his day as it is in ours. Jesus expanded this rule to include the entire web of activities involved in a murderous act. Not only is *murder* wrong, he said, but so is the *attitude* or *spirit* that motivates the murderous act (Matt. 5:21–22). Again, this is a harder principle to live by but one that will make a profound difference in the world if carried out.

Jesus's contribution, however, did not end with merely extending moral principles. He also established a movement of followers whom he called to live out these magnificent values as they went about telling others of God's love and forgiveness. Indeed, a deep commitment to teachings such as the Golden Rule was part of the very fabric of the life of his followers, since living them out is the way to uphold and honor the intrinsic dignity of all people.

Love and Social Justice

Since humans have intrinsic dignity, one would expect Jesus to urge respectful and loving treatment of others, and that is what we find. Loving one's neighbor as oneself, he said, was second in importance only to loving God himself. This moral principle is a recurring theme throughout the Scriptures, beginning very early in the Old Testament (Lev. 19:18) and continuing on to the end of the New Testament where James spells out what he calls the "royal law," which repeats the Leviticus passage, "Love your neighbor as yourself" (James 2:8).

The well-known story of the Good Samaritan (Luke 10:25–37) brings a practical dimension to this principle. It answers the question: How does one show love toward others day to day? The story was actually Jesus's response to a question from a member of his audience to whom we can be forever grateful. If this man had not asked his question, we may never have gotten this story. After hearing Jesus give this instruction, to love one's neighbor as oneself, the man asked him the potentially complicated question: "But who is my neighbor?"

After all, he reasoned, if we cannot define precisely who our neighbors are, how can there be an obligation to love them? Jesus's answer, in the form of this story, circumvented the objection by turning it on its head. The real question, it turns out, is not who our neighbors are but rather how *we can be neighbors* to the people around us.

The story is of a man from Samaria—an ethnic group with a long history of deep bitterness toward the Jews—who happened upon a Jewish man lying by the side of the road who had been beaten by thugs and left half dead. Even though two other travelers, both of them Jews, had already passed by on the other side of the road and ignored the man, the Samaritan went to help him. At great inconvenience to himself, and with a total disregard for ethnic hostilities, he stopped everything, anointed and bandaged up the man's wounds, and transported him to a place where he could get medical attention, which the Samaritan paid for.

After telling this story, Jesus turned to his audience and asked the very pointed question: "Which of these three, do you think, proved [*to be a*] *neighbor* to the man who fell among the robbers?" (Luke 10:36, italics mine). Of course the answer was obvious: the neighbor was the one who helped the man in need. Is anyone uncomfortable with that definition? Here again Jesus extended an already well-known moral principle and called his followers to practice it wherever they went.

Elsewhere Jesus said God looks with great favor on people who feed the hungry, give drink to those who are thirsty, practice hospitality, give clothes to those who need them, visit those in prison, comfort the bereaved, and assist people who are sick (Matt. 25:31–46). In the same passage he reserved some of his harshest words for those who refuse to carry out these acts of kindness.

While followers of Jesus have not always carried out these instructions as fully as they ought, many Christians have been deeply inspired by them and as a result have been moved on both small and large scales to carry out acts of compassion and social justice for people who are poor, homeless, sick, imprisoned, enslaved, or otherwise in need. Statistics Canada, the national statistical agency of that country, has pointed out that churchgoing Christians in Canada are generally much more likely than the majority of non-Christian Canadians to donate significantly to charities and to volunteer. According to their recent study, 62 percent of Canadians who regularly attend Christian services volunteered their time to various causes compared with only 43 percent of other Canadians. Surprisingly to some at least, these

Christians did not limit their giving to churches. Almost 60 percent of their volunteer time went to secular causes from health care to youth sports to various social and environmental organizations. Doug Todd, religion writer for the *Vancouver Sun* newspaper, summarizes the situation as revealed by Statistics Canada and his broader research this way:

> Christians are on the front lines, locally and around the globe, helping those who can not fend for themselves. They are supporting Canadian aboriginals, providing micro-loans in the Dominican Republic, handing out soup in Vancouver's Downtown Eastside, providing clean water in Ghana, ministering to people with AIDS and supporting environmental projects in Asia. . . . They've also led social justice movements: To free slaves, oppose wars, fight for civil rights or protect wilderness.[5]

As we will see later, many well-known organizations committed to social justice or compassion were brought into being by followers of Jesus as they carried out his command to feed the hungry, clothe the naked, and heal the sick.

The Moderation of Nationalism and the Reinforcement of Internationalism

Patriotism and nationalism are often viewed as positive sentiments, and why not? A sense of loyalty to one's people and country and a commitment to their well-being can bring strong cohesion and unity to any political state. Nationalism, however, has always had a dark side, especially when it has become excessive and militant, and this side has at times been very dark indeed. John Redekop goes so far as to declare that militant nationalism has been the scourge of humanity throughout history.[6] It has at times encouraged negative perceptions of members of other nations as outsiders, sometimes even as enemies, and such attitudes have all too often been the cause of bloody conflicts.

It may surprise some to learn that Christianity, when lived out consistently, reins in the tendency toward militant nationalism and brings it into a desperately needed balance. In the process, it also reinforces a wholesome international ethos. It does this in two ways. First, Christian teaching tells us that while earthly citizenship and the claims of one's country are important, they are always conditional. The apostle Paul made it clear that God established political authorities but did not give them unlimited power or purposes. They are identified as God's servants whose purpose is to work for the benefit of the people living within their jurisdiction (Rom. 13:1–7). Government is a bedrock institution of human affairs, intended by God to be a means of bringing civility, order, and peace where there might otherwise be chaos and bloodshed. It is against this background that Paul instructs his readers to submit to the authority of government as God's servants. It is a clear and insightful statement of the value, purpose, and limits God places upon human government.

Jesus's disciples explained this principle to the ruling authorities in Jerusalem by telling them that if their allegiance to *God* and to *government* ever came into conflict, they must choose obedience to God (Acts 4:19–20). Likewise, for anyone who takes biblical teaching seriously, citizenship in an earthly political state is always secondary, and patriotism is always qualified. This in no way minimizes the value of government. Even mediocre governments are able to prevent great amounts of chaos and suffering. British philosopher Thomas Hobbes aptly describes the state of living without government, commonly referred to as the State of Nature, as "solitary, poor, nasty, brutish, and short."[7] He is not far off.

A second way Christianity reinforces a wholesome international ethos is that excessive nationalism is reined in by the very nature of the Christian church. It is a transnational, global entity with members in every country and corner of the world. As such, it transcends all political boundaries. Christians often marvel over the immediate bond they feel upon meeting other Christians even from remote parts of the world. Political and cultural differences quickly fade in importance, and there is less of a tendency to see foreigners as outsiders or enemies, even those from countries at odds with our own. These are our brothers and sisters, first and foremost. The powerful effect is to promote international goodwill and a transnational understanding of people's concerns and challenges.

How, then, does one live the way Jesus calls us to? The answer is simple: by living according to the principles of human dignity, equality, the Golden Rule, the call to love others, and the moderation of militant nationalism. They are wonderful values, and Christianity promotes them wherever the teachings of Jesus are expressed and lived out. While no Christian has lived them out with complete consistency, many have taken them seriously, and it is time to see what they have given to the world as a result. David O. Moberg, professor of sociology at Marquette University, notes that "it has become fashionable in the academy and the public square to ignore or to deny the positive results of Christianity."[8] It is time for us to turn our attention to some of these results. They are gifts to the world that have flowed from the values taught in Christianity.

8

Christianity's Gifts to the World

Those who ardently desire the eradication of religion, particularly Christianity, would be well advised to carefully contemplate what they wish for. More precisely, they should reflect on what the world might be like if Christianity did not exist, or even what it was like before Jesus appeared on earth and his followers began living out his values.

An examination of history shows that not only is Christianity, when properly understood, innocent of the main allegations leveled against religion by its twenty-first-century critics, but it is the source of great good in the world. In fact, the beneficial impact of Christianity upon human civilization is nothing short of breathtaking. Unless you have previously investigated this question, I predict you will be surprised by what you are about to read. I hope you will also be as encouraged as I have been in doing this research.

The reality is that many of the good and humane things we in the West have come to take for granted and could hardly imagine the world without exist as a result of Christians simply living out the values Christ taught and in some cases doing so at great personal sacrifice. I have come to recognize this as an integral part of the response to the charge that Christianity is a dangerous force for evil and we would be better off without it. I contend that nothing could be further from the truth, and I will let the following brief examples speak for themselves.

Battling Infanticide

As we have seen, the earliest followers of Jesus held that human beings are made in God's image and, for this reason, human life is sacred and has intrinsic value. Because of this, they were understandably shocked at the low value placed upon the lives of humans, particularly the smallest and most vulnerable ones, by the people around them. Frederic Farrar has noted that "infanticide was infamously universal" among the Greeks and Romans.[1] Babies who were deformed or frail were especially at risk of being killed; often they were drowned, but sometimes more brutal methods were used. Infanticide was justified by key Roman and Greek thinkers and was so common that Polybius, a Greek historian who lived in the second century BC, blamed the population decline of ancient Greece on it.[2]

Unfortunately, this horrific practice has not been limited to ancient cultures. In the 1890s, missiologist and Princeton seminary lecturer James Dennis wrote that infanticide could also be found in many parts of Africa and was well known among the indigenous people of both North and South America.[3] Suffice it to say that we humans have a long and sorry history of being willing to kill our own young, defenseless children.

The early Christians labeled the practice of infanticide *murder*. In their minds, an infant had the same intrinsic worth as any other human being. In fact, they knew that Jesus had gone out of his way to shower special love on children (Matt. 19:14). Early Christian literature repeatedly condemned infanticide and commanded Christians not to practice it. The *Didache*, a document written between AD 85 and 110 representing the teaching of the disciples of Jesus, stated that the followers of Christ "shalt not . . . commit infanticide."[4] The *Epistle of Barnabas* likewise condemned this practice with the words, "You shall not abort a child nor, again, commit infanticide."[5]

Christians simply could not accept this immoral practice. To do so would have violated their foundational convictions concerning the value of human life, so they opposed it and worked to eliminate it wherever they went. Prior to the Edict of Milan in AD 313, which legally recognized Christianity, there was little Christians could do politically to abolish this practice. But once they were free to operate openly, it did not take them long to exert influence on the emperor, Valentinian. He was a Christian and was encouraged by Bishop Basil of Caesarea to officially outlaw infanticide. In AD 374 it finally happened.

While infanticide has never totally disappeared from our world, the Christian church has not wavered in its condemnation of it, and happily, moral sentiment against this practice has spread widely, with the result that laws against this practice are in effect in much of the world today. In the words of Alvin J. Schmidt, retired professor of sociology at Illinois College in Jacksonville, Illinois, the largely successful fight to end infanticide "is one of Christianity's greatest legacies."[6]

Struggle to End Child Abandonment

An equally abhorrent practice, although one far less known, was that of abandoning unwanted children. As Alvin Schmidt points out, if unwanted infants in the Greco-Roman world were not killed, they were frequently abandoned. This practice is mentioned repeatedly in early Greek and Roman literature, and incredibly, as Schmidt also notes, "in neither Greek nor Roman literature can one find any feelings of guilt related to abandoning children."[7]

As with infanticide, Christians from the highest levels of leadership on down condemned this practice, and for the same reasons. If humans, including children, are made in God's image, it means they have intrinsic worth and dignity, and abandoning them to die is wrong. Clement of Alexandria, an influential church father in Egypt in the last half of the second century, condemned the Romans for their contradictory moral practices in this regard. At the same time as they took great care to protect young birds and other animals, he said, they lacked any moral hesitation about abandoning their own children.[8] The African church father Tertullian also strongly denounced the practice of child abandonment.[9]

Christians, however, did much more than merely condemn this practice. As Schmidt notes, they took it upon themselves to rescue abandoned children, take them into their homes, adopt them, and raise them as their own children. One man named Callistus of Rome showed a particular passion for this cause by finding abandoned children and placing them in Christian homes. Benignus of Dijon, who lived in the late second century, also provided protection and nourishment for abandoned children, some of whom were deformed from failed abortions. Schmidt notes that Christian writings are replete with examples of Christians adopting children without homes.[10]

Their determined efforts eventually produced results when in AD 374, along with outlawing infanticide, Emperor Valentinian also criminalized the practice of infant abandonment. Subsequent emperors and kings followed, and this eventually brought about a shift in people's thinking concerning the morality of this practice. While it still occasionally occurs even today, it is normally regarded as tragic, and most societies attempt to rescue such babies. The largely successful battle against the practice of abandoning unwanted children is one of Christianity's gifts to the world's children.

Orphanages and Child Care

The care that early Christians gave to young, vulnerable children did not stop with their fight against such practices as infanticide and child abandonment. Life expectancy during Christianity's early years was short—often not much more than thirty years—and consequently many parents died, leaving their children as orphans. In fact, it was not uncommon for young children to have one or both parents die.[11] Christians understood the biblical mandate to care for these helpless orphans as well as other highly vulnerable people including widows, the sick, the disabled, and the poor. As the New Testament book of James puts it, "Religion that God our Father accepts as pure and faultless is this: to look after orphans and widows in their distress" (James 1:27 NIV). From the earliest days of the church, Christians followed this mandate and took pity on orphans, beginning with the practice of requiring godparents to be present at a child's baptism where they promised to care for the child in the event that he or she was orphaned. This custom gave children a second level of protection.[12]

As early as the first half of the second century, Justin Martyr, one of the first Christian apologists, pointed out in his *Apology* that collections were taken in church services to help orphans.[13] Tertullian, another Christian apologist and church father, revealed that the church in Carthage, Africa, had a common treasury "to aid the boys and girls who have neither fortune nor parents."[14] The *Apostolic Constitutions*, which was compiled between AD 350 and 400 and is the most comprehensive and best-preserved collection of ecclesiastical law we have from the early church, describes ways in which Christian bishops sought help for orphans.[15]

After Christianity was legalized in AD 313, Christians built institutions known as *orphanatrophia* (literally, "to care for orphans") and *brephotrophia* (literally, "to care for children") to provide organized care for young children. These institutions marked the formal beginning of orphanages, which eventually became common throughout the world. By the middle and latter part of the fourth century, St. Basil of Caesarea and St. Chrysostom of Constantinople were calling for the construction of *orphanatrophia*, which were commonly built alongside cathedrals.[16] Over the next few centuries, various Christian religious orders began to provide care for orphans. One such order was the Order of the Holy Ghost, which by the end of the thirteenth century was operating more than eight hundred homes for orphans. Many monasteries also cared for orphans during the Middle Ages.[17]

Over the centuries, orphanages supported by Christian giving continued to spread throughout Europe, and many individual Christians went further, founding and operating orphanages themselves. A. H. Francke, a Lutheran pastor and professor at Halle University in Germany in the late seventeenth century, was one such person. As part of his work, he both taught and provided orphan care for homeless young people. George Müller was another: an English evangelist and philanthropist in the nineteenth century, he founded a home for orphaned girls in the city of Bristol, England, where he was working as a missionary to the Jews. His work for orphans spread to other British cities, and by the time he died in 1898 more than eight thousand children were being cared for and educated in numerous orphanages connected to his organization.[18]

One other practice undertaken by Christians on behalf of vulnerable children is worthy of mention, namely that of orphan trains. Not all orphans in the Middle Ages or later found their way into orphanages. Some became vagrants, and it was these young people who motivated American clergyman Charles Loring Brace, who served with the Congregational Church, to found the Children's Aid Society in 1853. Brace believed that these young children would be best served if they could be rescued from their hopeless condition and live with an American farm family. There they would experience normal family life; get fresh air, guidance, and good food; and learn the value of productive work. Hundreds of these young vagrants were placed on trains, which came to be called *orphan trains*, and sent to farm families in upstate New York, Connecticut, New Jersey, and the Midwest.[19]

It is significant that the establishment of orphanages, the practice of godparents at child baptisms, and orphan trains for the care of young vagrant children were all Christian innovations. Alvin Schmidt bluntly states,

> Thousands upon thousands of unwanted infants were rescued by the early Christians and given the chance to attain a normal life all because Jesus Christ had inspired his followers to heed his words: "I was a stranger and you invited me in" (Matt. 25:35) and "Let the little children come to me, and do not hinder them, for the kingdom of God belongs to such as these" (Mark 10:14).[20]

Salvation Army

Few international organizations are as highly regarded around the world as the Salvation Army. To this day, members of this organization continue to go quietly about their work of visiting people in hospitals, assisting poor families, providing food, beds, and sometimes work for the homeless and unemployed, and giving counsel and other assistance to the most unfortunate members of society.

As its name reflects, the Salvation Army has a Christian origin and is another of Christianity's gifts to the world. It was founded by a young pastor in London named William Booth, who in the 1860s, after reading and preaching the words of Jesus to his congregation week by week, was moved to act on those teachings by combating the poverty, disease, and crime he saw in London's East End. In 1865 he began a ministry first known as the East London Christian Revival, which was supported by several Christian philanthropists. One of the first actions of the new ministry was to establish a program known as Food-for-a-Million, which provided meals for the poor at reasonable prices. The first annual conference of the new mission was held in November 1870. Over the next eight years this ministry evolved, until in August 1878 the Salvation Army was officially formed.[21]

The Salvation Army continued to expand its work, targeting the most vulnerable and troubled members of society. In 1883 it opened a halfway house for released prisoners in Melbourne, Australia, and in 1884 it began the bold work of helping young girls escape from the slave trade into which they had been sold. By 1886 the Army had moved to Canada and opened up an institution to help alcoholic women in

Toronto. By 1889 Salvation Army workers were busy opening shelters for the homeless wherever they found them.[22]

Today this organization continues to attract a legion of volunteers and paid personnel, some of whom are not Christians. Its focus remains largely the same, providing compassion and assistance to society's most needy members: the poor, unemployed, sick, and homeless. Furthermore, due to the experience and skill the Army has gained in providing this kind of assistance, many other organizations, including churches and governments, regularly contribute financially to it, enabling it to carry on its work. It is a story of compassionate activism for which we can all be thankful.

YMCA and YWCA

Most of us are familiar with the Young Men's Christian Association, known today simply as the YMCA, even if we are not fully informed of the wide range of beneficial activities this organization has performed over the years. But how many of us know that it was formerly called Draper's Evangelical Union or that it was formed in the early 1840s by an Englishman named George Williams as a way of channeling his commitment to Jesus Christ? Its original purpose was to help young men who were coming to London from the rural areas of England to find work in the big city. Often they were turning to low and degrading forms of sensuality, and Williams's initial stated mission in forming this organization was "to improve the spiritual condition of young men engaged in the drapery and other trades"; hence the name, Draper's Evangelical Union.[23]

In 1844 the name was changed to "Young Men's Christian Association," and in 1851 the YMCA came to North America, beginning in Boston and Montreal, where it grew rapidly. It soon broadened its objectives and activities to include such projects as providing inexpensive temporary lodging in YMCA hotels for young men who were searching for jobs or simply traveling from one city to another. Today, these "Y" hotels can be found in many major cities in North America.[24]

Although young women were always welcome to join the YMCA, they chose to form their own group in London in 1855. The initial goal of this group was to find housing for nurses who returned from the Crimean War, but its activities soon broadened. An American counterpart was formed in 1858, first known as the Ladies' Christian

Association. In 1868 its name was changed to the Young Women's Christian Association.[25]

Today, even though both groups retain the word *Christian* in their official names, neither of them is an explicitly Christian organization nor does either group require members to be affiliated with a Christian church, as was the case when they were founded. Nevertheless, Christianity gifted the world with both organizations. They are simply two more ways that Christians, following the mandates of their faith, extended charity to meet needs they saw around them, and the world is a better place because they did.

Red Cross

The Red Cross is another organization that was begun due to Christian influences. It was founded in 1864 by Jean Henri Dunant, a native of Switzerland who was the son of a wealthy banking family in Geneva and the first recipient of the Nobel Peace Prize. In spite of his privileged roots, he referred to himself as "a disciple of Christ as in the first century, and nothing more."[26] In 1859 he witnessed the suffering of wounded soldiers at the Battle of Solferino in Italy's struggle for unification. This experience was traumatic and life-changing for him, and he declared he would never be able to forget the eyes of the soldiers who wanted to kiss his hand. He and four associates along with twenty-four delegates from sixteen nations set out to form the International Red Cross.[27]

The initial purpose of the new organization was to console and bind up the wounds of soldiers hurt on the battlefield—a function it still performs with distinction around the world. In 1871 the Red Cross spread across the Atlantic and was officially founded in America with the efforts of Clara Barton, who had valiantly nursed soldiers in the American Civil War.

Dunant's faith in Christ apparently led him to choose the Christian cross, the symbol of Christ's suffering, death, and redemption of the world, as the organization's emblem. The significance of the symbol should not be missed. In 1876 the Islamic country of Turkey adopted the humanitarian idea of the Red Cross and deserves great credit for forming a parallel organization, but it changed the name and symbol to the Red Crescent. In other words, the Red Crescent is an outgrowth of the Red Cross and, in light of this, it seems fair to say that were it not for Christianity, not only would there be no Red Cross, but in all likelihood, no Red Crescent would exist either.

Hospitals and Health Care

Most of us can hardly imagine a world without hospitals and medical care. But as Alvin J. Schmidt points out, the world the Christians entered during the Greco-Roman era had a colossal void with respect to caring for the sick and dying.[28] Notice how Dionysius, a Christian bishop during the third century, describes the way the Romans and Greeks treated their sick ones during an Alexandrian plague in about AD 250: "[They] thrust aside anyone who began to be sick, and kept aloof even from their dearest friends, and cast the sufferers out upon the public roads half dead, and left them unburied, and treated them with utter contempt when they died."[29]

Contrast this with Dionysius's astonishing description of the way Christians tended to the sick, often at great peril to their own health: "Many of our brethren . . . did not spare themselves, but . . . visited the sick without thought of their own peril, and ministered to them assiduously and treated them for their healing in Christ, died from time to time most joyfully . . . drawing upon themselves their neighbors' diseases."[30]

This contrast has been noticed by historians. Howard Haggard writes, "When epidemics broke out, [the Romans] often fled in fear and left the sick to die without care."[31] He adds that the Romans regarded helping a sick person as a sign of human weakness whereas the early Christians were aware of the words of Jesus, particularly his parable of the Good Samaritan, and so they regarded helping the sick as serving not only *them* but *God* as well. All human beings have intrinsic dignity and are precious in God's sight regardless of their medical condition, and therefore sick people ought to be given the care they need. According to American historian Rodney Stark, this contrast in attitude and action was nothing short of revolutionary in that era.[32]

In fairness, we should note that it is probably technically incorrect to say that medical care was entirely absent when the church came into existence, but there is a lack of certainty on the subject. For example, there were three hundred shrines to the mythical Greek healing god, Aesculapius, and some have wondered whether they were actually hospitals. As Haggard points out, however, these shrines were not hospitals but only places where people could spend a single night in buildings near the shrines for religious reasons.[33] Writing on the origins of hospitals, George Gask and John Todd explain that the sick did indeed come to the shrines of the god Aesculapius, but not for medical treatment. Instead they came to have the god appear to them in a dream and reveal to them the treatment they ought to follow.[34] Gerhard Uhlhorn, an expert on ancient Christian charity in the nineteenth century, says that the buildings housing these people for the night were "only hospices for shelter, and not hospitals for care and attendance."[35]

Questions have also been raised as to whether certain Greek institutions called *iatreia* functioned as very early hospitals. David Riesman, writing on the practice of medicine in history, explains that sick people did indeed go to these *iatreia* to be diagnosed by physicians who prescribed medication for them, but they provided no nursing provisions.[36]

Ralph Jackson, in his recent book *Doctors and Diseases in the Roman Empire*, mentions a Roman facility called the *valetudinarian* and calls it a hospital.[37] As Alvin Schmidt notes, however, a number of historians have shown that these facilities treated only sick slaves, gladiators, and sometimes ailing soldiers. The sick common people, manual laborers, and the poor simply had no place to go for medical care.[38] In other words, whether we speak of the god Aesculapius, the *iatreia*, or the *valetudinaria*, none operated as hospitals in the twenty-first-century sense of the term or in the way that the institutions later started by early Christians did. As Howard Haggard says, charity hospitals for the poor and the general public did not exist until Christians introduced them.

For the first three centuries of the life of the Christian church, Christians lived under the threat of persecution and could do little to care for the poor and ill beyond taking them into their own homes. But in the fourth century when Christianity became legally recognized, Christians immediately moved to provide such care. At the Council of Nicea in AD 325, which was the first ecumenical council of the Christian church, bishops were directed to build hospitals in every city that had a cathedral.[39] These early hospitals, known as *xenodochia*, provided medical care for the sick, shelter for the poor, and also lodging for Christian pilgrims. From that time on, hospitals began to be built throughout Europe, and by the sixth century they had become a common part of monasteries.[40] By the mid-sixteenth century there were thirty-seven thousand Benedictine monasteries that cared for the sick.[41]

Over time Christians founded health care orders. One was the Order of Hospitallers, which recruited women for nursing the sick.[42] Another was the Hospitallers of St. Lazarus, which devoted itself primarily to nursing.[43] By the thirteenth century, most hospitals in Europe were under the direction of Christian bishops. While this is no longer true today, the initiative taken by early Christians to care for the sick was highly influential in creating an institution that today is not only appreciated but taken for granted. Indeed, it is hard to imagine the world without hospitals.

Abolition of Slavery

The practice of human slavery has a long and shameful history. Contrary to the widely held perception that slavery has been primarily a sin committed by white people against blacks, it was widely practiced in Africa and the Arab world before spreading to Europe.[44] Alvin Schmidt reports that during the time Jesus walked the earth, slaves made up an estimated 75 percent of the population in Athens and well over half of the Roman population.[45] Most kings, priests, and philosophers approved of slavery, and Aristotle, one of the most influential Greek philosophers, saw it as natural and just and declared that "a slave is a living tool, just as a tool is an inanimate slave. Therefore there can be no friendship with a slave as slave."[46]

In many ways, slaves were devalued as human beings. Property owners and freeborn persons did not stoop to manual labor, which was work to be performed by slaves. When modern-day tourists admire such works as the Appian Way, the Seven Wonders of the World, and even beautiful sculptures from the same period in the Middle East or Europe, one wonders if they realize they are viewing the products of slave labor.

Most of us will probably also be surprised to learn how recently slavery has been abolished in various parts of the world. While the United States banned this practice in 1865, Ethiopia continued until 1942, Saudi Arabia until 1962, Peru until 1964, and India until 1976. Africa's largest country, Sudan, continues the practice to the present day.[47]

Even though some Christians throughout history have occasionally attempted to use the Bible to justify the enslavement of certain races, this practice has always been anathema to a Christian way of thinking, which is evident from the earliest widespread Christian attitudes toward it. Schmidt lists Polycarp, the second-century bishop of Smyrna; Athenagoras, a second-century Christian philosopher; Clement of Alexandria and Origen, third-century church fathers; and St. Bonaventure in the thirteenth century as examples of prominent Christians who justified or approved of slavery. He labels them as erring Christians who, whether willfully or out of ignorance, ignored the words of both Paul and Jesus and allowed themselves to be influenced by the practices of the prevailing culture.[48] Lactantius, writing in the fourth century, represented Christian teaching on the matter accurately when he declared in his *Divine Institutes* that in God's eyes there were no slaves.[49] Writing in the same time period, St. Augustine viewed slavery as the product of sin and as contrary to God's plan for humanity.[50] Since all persons are purposeful creations of a loving God and made in his image, all human life is equally precious in God's sight and ought to be treated as such.

The short New Testament book of Philemon is instructive in revealing the New Testament's attitude toward slavery. In it, Paul instructs the slave owner Philemon to no longer treat his runaway slave, Onesimus, as a slave at all but rather as a brother in Christ (Philem. 15–16). This was revolutionary. Whoever heard of treating slaves with dignity and humanity, as brothers and sisters for whom property owners provided employment and housing? This in effect amounted to a call to cease the practice of slavery.

In a similar vein, Paul tells the Christians living in the region of Galatia that from a Christian point of view "there is neither Jew nor Greek, there is neither slave nor free, there is neither male nor female; for you are all one in Christ Jesus" (Gal. 3:28). These two passages in the New Testament, undergirded as they are by the conviction that all human life has intrinsic dignity, laid the foundation for a deep opposition to slavery.

Christians began their struggle against slavery by simply demonstrating a radically different attitude toward slaves. As historian and Fellow of the British Academy, W. E. H. Lecky reports that the early Christians interacted with slaves in the same way as they did with freemen and carried on conversations with them at the same altar. In other words, they implicitly accepted and regarded them as having the same worth and dignity as freemen. This honor and acceptance resulted in many slaves embracing the new faith and some even becoming priests of the church. Most impressive in this regard is the third-century story of Callistus, a former slave who not only became a priest but later a bishop as well. In fact, the church lists him as one of its early popes.[51]

Christians went further, however, and began the practice of freeing slaves one by one as they had opportunity. Oxford historian Robin Lane Fox, a specialist in the relationship between the pagan and early Christian religions of the Roman Empire, reports that this act of granting freedom was often performed in a church in the presence of the bishop.[52] It is impossible to know how many slaves were freed this way during the early years of Christianity, but according to Lecky, there were many. He writes,

> St. Melania was said to have emancipated 8,000 slaves, St. Ovidius, a rich martyr of Gaul, 5,000, Chromatius, a Roman prefect under Diocletian, 1,400, Hermes, a prefect under Trajan, 1,200. [And] many of the Christian clergy at Hippo under the rule of St. Augustine, as well as great numbers of private individuals, freed their slaves as an act of piety.[53]

In AD 315, only two years after the Edict of Milan, the Christian emperor Constantine took the small step of criminalizing the act of stealing children for the purpose of bringing them up as slaves. Over the next few centuries, Christian bishops and councils called for the redemption and freeing of slaves, and Christian monks freed many themselves.[54] The effects were stunning. By the twelfth century slaves in Europe were rare, and by the fourteenth century they were almost unknown on that continent, including in England.[55]

Unfortunately, slavery was revived by the British in the seventeenth century. Ignoring a London church council decision of 1102 that outlawed the practice, the British began rounding up slaves in Africa and transporting them to England, its colonies in the West Indies, and America.[56] The Portuguese and Spanish also went to Africa for slaves and shipped them to their own colonies in Brazil, Central America, and parts of South America. The most lamentable element of this revival of the slave trade was that it was carried out by countries and people who commonly identified themselves as Christians. In these countries, Christianity had obviously become a cultural phenomenon with the teachings of Jesus having little impact on the values and day-to-day living habits of the citizens. But some serious Christians again saw slavery as a gross violation of the Christian belief in the equal and inherent dignity of all human beings, and they came to the forefront in the battle against it all over again.

One giant stands out, namely William Wilberforce (1759–1833). As a long-serving member of the British Parliament, he fought to change the heart of his nation. He strove against the entrenched powers and economic structures of his society and was ultimately successful not merely in winning his specific battle—to end slavery—but in kindling the consciences of the people of his society to the need for justice in other areas as well. The far-reaching effects of his efforts are seen, in part, in the way Western civilization today views slavery. In Wilberforce's day the practice was commonplace; today it is unthinkable.

The story of Wilberforce is worth briefly telling. He had a privileged background and from his youth demonstrated considerable personal skills. His humor and wit gained him friends easily, and his intelligence and skill as a debater and orator made him highly successful as a parliamentarian. He was said to have been able to speak to an audience for hours and make people enjoy it. As a young man he had no use for religion and consequently fit well into the social scene of London. The city, described as one vast casino in Wilberforce's time, was known for its prestigious private clubs, gambling casinos, brothels, and prostitutes who specialized in any manner of perversion one wanted.

This luxurious, decadent lifestyle was underwritten by child labor and the slave trade, which had become not only successful businesses but also national policies. The slave trade was supported by planters and gentlemen who had grown rich through the profits of their trade and then had used these profits to become an increasingly powerful force in Parliament. They would pay up to five thousand pounds to buy boroughs that sent their representatives to the House of Commons. Few practices were more entrenched in the economic structure of England than slavery. Challenging it seemed hopeless, although a few religious groups tried. But the nation had yet to feel the impact of William Wilberforce.

Through the urging of his old schoolmaster Isaac Milner, Wilberforce agreed to read the Christian Scriptures daily. As his diary from 1785 indicates, he began to feel increasingly dissatisfied with his current condition. A dramatic turning point came when he was led to Christ by John Newton, who had been held in bondage by the Royal Navy and then had become a Christian while working as a slave trader.

But what did it mean to be a Christian, especially as a member of Parliament in the eighteenth century? Wilberforce pondered that question and soon came to the conviction that though his conversion meant that God had eternally rescued his soul, the meaning must go deeper. True Christianity not only saves but serves, he believed. It must bring God's compassion to the oppressed. It must, in fact, oppose the oppressors.

Through the influence of the brilliant essayist and clergyman Thomas Clarkson, whose pamphlets detailed the brutality of the slave trade, Wilberforce's social conscience was kindled. In 1787 he wrote, "Almighty God has set before me two great objectives: the abolition of the slave trade and the reformation of manners (i.e., morals)."[57] With those words he began an epic struggle against slavery, along with a number of other entrenched evils in English society including debtor laws and child labor. This struggle did not end until a few days before his death on July 26, 1833, when Wilberforce received word that Parliament had passed the Abolition Act that he had presented to Parliament in 1823. This law resulted in England freeing seven hundred thousand slaves in its West Indies colonies.[58] Largely as a result of his efforts, and those working with him, slavery came to a complete end in all of the British Empire by 1840. It was the first modern country to outlaw slavery; others were soon to follow.[59]

William Wilberforce still stands as an inspiration to Christians around the world who continue the struggle for social justice for oppressed people. He is an example of a success story in this struggle. Why did he succeed? When one looks at his life, his passion for oppressed people, and the strategies he employed to bring about justice for them, there are a number of lessons that can contribute to our effectiveness in bringing about social change in our own culture. These have been laid out and analyzed elsewhere, and we would be unwise to ignore them.[60]

Establishing Universities

As we have stated repeatedly, from the earliest days of Christianity, followers of Christ have believed in human dignity and the equal worth of all human beings. This conviction is founded on the belief that humans are purposeful creations of a loving God who made them in his image. Part of this image of God in humans includes the power of reason—the ability to think and to be self-aware. This is why there have always been Christians who are committed to the development and cultivation of the mind. It started with Jesus, who was known not only as a healer and Redeemer but also as a teacher—and an exceedingly great one at that. The early apostles, the direct students of Jesus whom he commissioned to continue his work, also carried on a teaching ministry. In fact, as Luke puts it, "They never stopped teaching" (Acts 5:42 NIV). And later, when Paul set out the qualifications for being a bishop (meaning an overseer and leader) in the very early church, one was that the bishop be "able to teach" (1 Tim. 3:2 NIV).

The early church continued its emphasis on teaching by establishing teaching documents or manuals from very early on. One of the most well known was the *Didache*, which was essentially an instruction manual for new members of the Christian community. This and other documents were used in the catechetical instruction given to young converts to the faith. Over time the practice of providing this instruction developed into catechetical schools that had a strong literary emphasis. These schools began to spring up wherever Christians went, and by about AD 150 Justin Martyr, who is sometimes referred to as the Christian church's first great scholar, had established catechetical schools in Ephesus and Rome. While the teaching of Christian doctrine was the primary focus, some schools, such as the one in Alexandria, also taught mathematics and medicine. When Origen succeeded Clement at Alexandria, he went further and added grammar classes to the curriculum.[61]

This emphasis on education was later instrumental in the formation of monasteries, which became, in part, learning centers. Alvin J. Schmidt calls them "embryonic universities" and notes that while they were not full-fledged universities as we know them today in that their primary goal was to train monks and priests, they provided the academic footing for their later development.[62] For this reason, Rodney Stark calls the university a Christian invention. The first two universities appeared in Paris, where both Albert Magnus and Thomas Aquinas taught, and Bologna in the middle of the twelfth century.[63] Oxford and Cambridge were founded around 1200 followed by a flood of new institutions during the remainder of the thirteenth century: Toulouse, Orleans, Naples, Salamanca, Seville, Lisbon, Grenoble, Padua, Rome, Perugia, Pisa, Modena, Florence, Prague, Cracow, Vienna, Heidelberg, Cologne, Ofen, Erfurt, Leipzig, and Rostock.[64]

As George Marsden, specialist in American religion and culture and professor of history at the University of Notre Dame, asserts, from their earliest beginnings of monastic roots through to the nineteenth century, all universities were founded as Christian institutions regardless of whether they taught law, theology, or medicine and all operated within theological boundaries.[65]

The university as an institution devoted exclusively to higher learning was something new in the world. It was not a monastery or place for meditation. The new medieval universities were not like Christian monasteries or Chinese academies for training Manadrins or Zen masters' schools. They were primarily concerned not with passing on the received wisdom but with innovative thinking, and it was this kind of new thinking that was rewarded with fame and invitations to teach elsewhere.[66]

Christian influence on higher education carried over into North America. Given the strongly secular nature of most universities and colleges in North America today, many North Americans would be surprised to know that in 1932, when Donald Tewksbury published his work entitled *The Founding of American Colleges and Universities before the Civil War*, 92 percent of the 182 colleges and universities in existence were founded by Christian denominations. Most of the well-known colleges and universities in North America today began as Christian schools. Harvard College, established in 1636, now known as Harvard University, was founded by the Congregational Church; the College of William and Mary began as an Episcopalian school principally to train clergy; and Yale University began primarily as a Congregational school with its stated mission being to "Educate Ministers in Our Own Way."[67] Northwestern University in Evanston, Illinois, was founded by the Methodists; Columbia University, first known as King's College, was started by the Episcopalian Church; and Princeton University began as a Presbyterian school. Even some state universities such as the University of Kentucky, the University of California Berkeley, and the University of Tennessee had origins as church schools.[68]

The Christian stamp on colleges and universities is often evidenced by their names, which were commonly given in honor of Christian saints: St. Anne, St. Anthony, St. Mary, St. Bernard, St. Olaf, and so on. Others were given names such as: Christ, Trinity, Emmanuel, King's, and Magdalene. Schools with names like these would not be in existence today had it not been for the Christian faith.

Christianity's Continuing Positive Influence

"As an atheist, I truly believe Africa needs God: Missionaries, not aid money, are the solution to Africa's biggest problem—the crushing passivity of the people's mindset." With these astonishing words, atheist Matthew Parris sums up the conclusion he was forced to draw after visiting the African country of Malawi, his childhood home.

Parris spent his childhood in the African country of Malawi, and forty-five years after leaving, he decided to return due to his interest in Pump Aid, a British charity that helps rural African communities install water pumps, giving them access to clean water. Not only did this visit renew his faith in development charities, it also caused a crisis of faith for him. As an atheist, he found the enormous contribution to the good of Africa stemming from Christian evangelism perplexing. He was not able to harmonize it with his atheism, but in the end he admitted it was real and unlike any other form of aid or developmental work being carried out in Malawi.

In particular, he found the evangelism of Christians to be distinctly different from the work of secular nongovernmental organizations and government endeavors. As good as the work done by these secular organizations is, he declares, it will never be sufficient, nor will education and training. The difference Christianity offers, he says, is a change of people's hearts. "It brings a spiritual transformation. The rebirth is real. The change is good."

This marks a significant difference in Parris's perspective. He used to argue that while the humanitarian work Christians did in Africa was good—building schools, hospitals, clean water systems, and so on—it is the fact that people are helped that is important, not the faith of those doing the work. He doesn't say that anymore. Such an attitude does not fit the facts he has witnessed. He has now found that faith does more than simply motivate people to good deeds. It transfers to others, and the effects are immense.

He remembers as a child having Christian missionaries stay in their family home. They were always different, he says. "Their faith appeared to have liberated and relaxed them. There was a liveliness, a curiosity, an engagement with the world—a directness in their dealings with others—that seemed to be missing in traditional African life." He specifically recalls a trip with four friends by Land Rover from Algiers to Nairobi, Kenya, at the age of twenty-four. Their search for a safe bed at night often resulted in them locating near a Christian mission, and he remembers that when entering an area containing missionaries, something changed in the people they met. They approached you directly, person-to-person, without looking down or away, he recalls.

On his recent trip "home" to Malawi, he discovered to his surprise that "a handful of the most impressive African members of the Pump Aid team (largely from Zimbabwe) were, privately, strong Christians." Their honesty, diligence, and optimism in their work deeply impressed Parris, and he would have been willing to see it all disconnected from their personal faith, but that assessment did not seem to fit the facts either. Their perception of self, he said, is founded on their belief in humanity's place in the universe—something that Christianity teaches.[69]

We can argue against the details of a testimony like Matthew Parris's, but it is his story. It stands as a testimony to the continuing deep, positive influence of Christianity wherever it goes.

9

Is There a Way Forward?

True Religion

A very practical question remains: Where do we go from here? Are there solutions or at least constructive steps we can take toward solving the problem of religious violence? Is there a way forward? This is an urgent question that defies simplistic answers. One thing seems clear: eradicating religion from the world, even if such a thing were possible, offers no hope of ending the violence—even the religious violence. In fact, as we have seen, the attempt to do away with religion has been behind some of the worst violence our world has ever experienced. What is more, as we also discovered, many acts of violence that *appear* to be religiously motivated are actually driven by deeper political, cultural, or ideological motivations that would remain even if religion were gone.

Sadly, religion is sometimes turned into a tool used by perpetrators of violence to help recruit "soldiers" to carry out their vicious acts. This constitutes a heinous abuse of religion, and the vast majority of religious people are outraged by this violence done in the name of religion. Most, in fact, are personally offended by being lumped into the same group as those carrying out such vicious acts.

But we must remember that religion is not the only ideal or ideology that can be abused and turned toward evil purposes. Other alternatives exist such as liberty, equality, community, tolerance, and even atheism. We noted earlier that when a society becomes secularized, it will tend to elevate any number of alternative nonreligious ideals to the level of what Alister McGrath calls "quasi-divine authorities" that no one is permitted to challenge. In such a situation, these ideals become ripe for abuse. We drew attention to the example of Madame Rolande from the French Revolution, who was brought to the guillotine in 1792 to face execution on trumped-up charges. This insightful woman bowed mockingly to the statue of liberty and uttered the words: "Liberty, what crimes are committed in your name."[1]

This has serious implications. If all ideals are susceptible to being misused to promote violence, it means the root problem is deeper than any single ideal. Therefore, rather than lashing out at any particular ideal as if it were the wellspring of the violence, we need to figure out how to prevent the abuse of such ideals. Anything less misses the mark and leaves the root problem untouched.

But how does one pinpoint the root problem? Where does one search for it? Here is where things get interesting, because if the analysis in this book is correct, the root problem may be closer than we think—uncomfortably close. Since it is humans who have abused any number of ideals throughout history, it is hard to avoid the conclusion that the root of the problem lies with us, or should I say *within* us.

Perhaps G. K. Chesterton understood this better than most when he wrote his essay for *The Times*, a newspaper published in the United Kingdom. The paper had invited several prominent authors to submit essays on the question, "What's Wrong with the World?" Chesterton's submission was in the form of a letter that read only:

> Dear Sirs,
>   I am.
>   Sincerely yours,
>   G. K. Chesterton[2]

He understood something we all know deep down—that the source of the world's most intractable problems lies within us humans and not somewhere *out there*. If so, any solution to these problems will have to involve a change within us. But is such a change possible? Can you and I really become something new and different from what we are? This is a profound question that philosophers and theologians have pondered for hundreds of years. Interestingly, such change from within is precisely what Jesus of Nazareth came to offer the world. As a Christian, I find this both fascinating and deeply encouraging.

Admittedly there is a touch of irony at the mention of Jesus. It means we have come full circle in this discussion. After beginning this book by seeing the accusing finger pointed directly at religion as the cause of the world's deepest problems, we may now need to turn to something—or should I say *someone?*—who might sound very religious to us, namely Jesus of Nazareth, not as the *source* of the problems but as their *solution*. If change from within is what we need, we would be unwise to ignore his words.

The historical sources that tell us about him, the four Gospels of the New Testament, speak of the change he came to bring. They tell us that in Jesus a new kind of person appeared with a new kind of life that he offers to impart to us. He was unlike any person who had ever walked on this earth. In him, the Creator of the universe became not only a man but a baby, and before that a fetus inside a woman's body. Incredibly, he came to make his own life available to be put into us if we choose to let him. In fact, he desires to live his life in and through our lives so that, in a sense, it is no longer really we who live but Christ living his life through us. It is his way of making us something radically new and different.

It's an astonishing story, and there may be a hesitation to trust the books that tell it. After all, aren't they just religious writings? There is our question about religion again. We must recognize, however, that if we write off these books simply because they are found in the Bible, we will be committing one of the most elementary errors in logic: the *genetic fallacy*. When we reject or disregard an idea because of its origin, we commit this fallacy. The *truth* of an idea is a different matter than its *origin*, and we must evaluate ideas on their own merit.

This is particularly important in the case of the four Gospels since they are historical documents written with the express purpose of giving us information about the life, times, and teachings of Jesus. And we have exceptionally strong reasons for regarding them as reliable history. Their writers claimed to be eyewitnesses who were either the very disciples of Jesus or directly connected to them, thus giving them close access to Jesus. Furthermore, the Gospels are dated very close to the time of the events they describe—within twenty-five to forty years—which left insufficient time for legendary development to occur and be projected back onto the life of Jesus.[3]

These documents also contain a number of internal indicators of authenticity (which we discussed in chapter 4). Particularly important is the use of women as the primary witnesses to the most important parts of the story of Jesus: his burial and empty tomb (Luke 23:55–24:10). Given the lowly status of women in first-century Palestine, using women in this way would be unthinkable for anyone fabricating a story they wanted others to believe, especially when men (i.e., the disciples of Jesus) were available to be used. Almost as important is identification of Joseph of Arimethea as the man who asked permission to take the body of Jesus down from the cross and bury it in his own tomb (Luke 23:50–53). No one fabricating this kind of story would include such a person in his narrative because he was a prominent member of the Sanhedrin—something of a supreme court for the Jewish people at the time—and it would be too easy to do a quick fact-check and prove the whole thing was made up.

Beyond all of this is the obvious willingness of the writers of these documents to tell the story of Jesus and his followers, warts and all. They did not hide details that were embarrassing or unflattering. In one case the disciples—the future leaders in the early Christian move-ment—are shown arguing about which of them will be the greatest in the kingdom of God (Mark 9:33–35). Another time Peter is reported promising never to deny Jesus and then, literally within hours, going out and doing precisely that three times in a row, swearing and cursing to make his point (Matt. 26:35, 69–75). This is not a pretty picture, but it is a realistic picture of the life and teachings of Jesus that ap-pears eminently trustworthy.

The first thing you encounter when you read this story about Jesus is a dilemma, namely a problem of reconciling two seemingly incom-patible ideas. The first is the depth and overall excellence of his moral teaching, which is hardly questioned even by opponents of Christianity. In fact, we have all heard people prefix their criticisms of Christianity with words like, "Oh, don't get me wrong, I'm in agreement with the moral teachings of Jesus. He was a great moral teacher." They are right. In his teachings morality is exhibited at its deepest and best.

The other idea concerns the astonishing nature of the claims Jesus made concerning himself, not just on one or a few occasions but regularly and in a variety of contexts. He claimed to be the unique Son of God, on one occasion taking the well-known name for God, "I am," for himself (John 8:58). This claim was correctly understood by his Jewish audience to be a claim to equality with God, and they immediately tried to stone him for blasphemy. He never pretended they were incorrect, even to avoid stoning. On another occasion he told his followers that he was the one who throughout the centuries had been sending wise men and leaders into the world (Matt. 23:34–37). On still another, he asserted that, as the Son of God, he would appear at the end of history as the judge of the world (Matt. 25:31–46).

In the meantime, he offered to forgive the sins of those he spoke with, and not merely the sins that were done against him, but all their sins (Mark 2:5–12). This is such an outrageous claim that it is easy to miss its significance. We know that if we offend our neighbor and later ask him or her for forgiveness, it is in our neighbor's power to grant us forgiveness if he or she so chooses. But what would we think of a person who announces that he or she forgives you for committing an offense against your neighbor. Jesus did exactly this quite regularly. As C. S. Lewis puts it, Jesus behaved as if he is the party primarily concerned and offended in all offenses, and this makes sense only if he really is the God whose laws are broken and whose love is wounded in every sin.[4]

Here is the dilemma. Rich and sane moral teachings were given by the same person who made claims that, if not true, were those of an egomaniac virtually unequalled in the world. If true, however, Jesus was absolutely unique, and we would be wise to take him seriously. There is no parallel in other religions or anywhere else. The things he said are very different from the teachings of any other teacher. Others point us *to* the truth while Jesus says, "I *am* the way, and the truth, and the life" (John 14:6, italics mine).

We must decide what we will do with this information about Jesus. Interestingly, the one option not open to us is the very one many people today prefer, and that is believing that Jesus was a great moral teacher but nothing more. No mere human who made the kind of claims Jesus made for himself would be a great moral teacher. He would, at best, be mentally deranged or, at worst, a malicious liar. How more villainous could you be than to gain followers and promise them eternal life that you know you can never grant? If we read the documents, we will see that his immediate hearers never regarded him as a mere moral teacher. People either hated him and wanted him dead, feared him and kept their distance, or adored him and worshiped him as God. We each have to make our own choice as well.

Jesus's followers from the earliest times until today have consistently declared that he is exactly who he claimed to be: the eternal Creator of the universe revealed in human form who came to impart new life to the people of this world. He desires to live his life in and through us. This Christ-life inside us, as C. S. Lewis calls it, puts us

in an entirely different position than we were in before. We become
the organism through which he acts in this world—his fingers, arms,
and muscles. In the process of operating through us, Christ makes us
radically different people, "new creatures" to use Paul's language. It is
a revolutionary concept, and it leads to a change that is crucial if we
ever hope to find a solution to the problem of violence and cruelty in
our broken world. When we are rightly related to God by having the
Christ-life within us, our relations with the human beings around us
change too. C. S. Lewis illustrates this with the picture of the relationship of spokes in a wheel to the hub and to each other. When the
spokes are fitted correctly into the hub and the rim, they are bound
to be in the right relationship to each other as well.[5]

Apart from the Christ-life operating within us, however, we are
simply bankrupt when it comes to living virtuously in our relations
with others. We can see this in an instant by simply asking ourselves
whether we treat others the way we know we ought to—the way we
would like them to treat us. How well do we live up to even our own
moral ideals, not to mention those of a morally perfect God? The
harder we try, the more we fail. In fact, that is precisely how we discover our failure to live up to our ideals, by trying our hardest to live
as we know we should and then discovering we do not make it. When
this point arrives, Jesus calls us simply to turn to him and say, "You
must do this because I cannot." This kind of change may happen in
a flash or it may be so gradual that you cannot point to a particular
moment. What matters is that we leave it to Christ to somehow share
with us the perfect life he carried out while on earth, to somehow
make us more like himself.

This may be difficult to understand. The idea that the Uncreated
Eternal Being, the God from outside nature, comes down into nature and shares his life with us is going to be hard to grasp. But just
as a person can take a breath without knowing how the oxygen is
processed by the lungs and sent into the bloodstream, in the same
way a person can accept what Christ has done without knowing
how it all works.

But can we be sure that people who follow Christ will reject violence
and injustice? After all, haven't people who claimed to follow Christ
been guilty of some of the very crimes and injustices we have been
dealing with in this book? Perhaps we ourselves have had bad experiences with some of Jesus's followers—our neighbors, colleagues, or
business associates who were unkind, dishonest, or hypocritical even

as they claimed to follow Christ. Why, then, should we think following Christ will bring the difference we seek?

This question is relevant, and the first thing to say is that we are imperfect humans with a long way to go. None of us will change all at once. It will be a process, and along the way we will not always measure up to the life Jesus is growing inside us. Second, it would be a mistake to reject what Jesus promises to do for us because some people who claim he did it for them continue to live the same old way. We should never judge things by their abuse. Furthermore, for all we know, they may be more loving, gentle, honest, and kind than they would be if the life of Jesus was not growing in them.

Most importantly, we should ask how we would like to have Jesus himself as a neighbor. This is important because it is Jesus whom we are called to follow and who promises to impart his life to us. He had no moral flaws, nor did he inflict violence on anyone. In this book about violence done in the name of religion, it is imperative to emphasize that while Jesus was the object of violence, he was never the initiator of it. He ultimately ended up being crucified for crimes he did not commit. Instead of meeting violence with violence or anger with anger, Jesus called upon his followers to turn the other cheek, go the second mile, and not let the sun go down on their anger. It is this kind of life he desires to put into us, and when he does, our thinking will be transformed bit by bit to become like his. That is why his true followers over the past two thousand years have been shocked and outraged when people use violence as a means to achieve their religious aims on earth. They are no more shocked than Jesus himself is. Violence is not the way of Jesus, and it is not the way of his true followers.

Jesus went even further than merely avoiding violence. He called his followers to love their neighbors and then extended this well-known command in two striking ways. First, he said loving our neighbors, with whom we share much in common, is a good start, but we must go further. We must love our enemies too (Matt. 5:44). Isn't it hard enough just to love our neighbors?

Second, in the parable of the Good Samaritan (Luke 10:30–37), which we discussed earlier in this book, Jesus changed the question, indeed the entire equation, in what it means to love our neighbors. The real question, he said, is not *who are my neighbors* so I can love them, but rather, *how can I be a neighbor to all people, especially to those on the outside of my in-group?* That is the entire point of this famous story, and it left his critics without reply. Jesus then lived out this principle himself, demonstrating for us what it means to love and be neighborly to those who are different, who are not part of our group. As a result, one of the main criticisms leveled against Jesus by his opponents was that he accepted and touched people who were considered by his culture to be unclean: sinners, tax collectors, and prostitutes (Matt. 8:3; 9:20–25; 21:31–32; Luke 15:1–2). He welcomed these marginalized groups and was an anomaly among his contemporaries for doing so. Christians can be accused of failing to live up to this ideal, but there it is, right at the core of Jesus's teaching. We must remember what Jesus taught us in passages such as Matthew 5:44–47 (paraphrased):

> Everyone can be kind to their friends—love must do more.
> Love your enemies and pray for those who persecute you!
> This is how true children of God act.

Notes

Chapter 1 The Power of Religion

1. Sam Harris, *The End of Faith: Religion, Terror, and the Future of Reason* (New York: W. W. Norton, 2005), 11.

2. Ibid., 11–12.

3. Ibid., 26.

4. Ibid., 133.

5. Ibid., 26.

6. Ibid., 13.

7. An important caveat: As will be made clear throughout the book, I believe it is inaccurate to label all violent acts for which the perpetrators claim a religious impetus as "religious violence." I use the term only as a reference to what the new critics mistakenly call these acts of violence and to avoid the laboriousness of reexplaining this discrepancy each time the term appears in the text.

8. Richard Dawkins, *God Delusion* (Boston: Houghton Mifflin, 2006), 31.

9. Jerry Adler, "The New Naysayers," *Newsweek*, 11 September 2006, 47–49.

10. Daniel C. Dennett, *Breaking the Spell: Religion as a Natural Phenomenon* (New York: Penguin Books, 2006), 4.

Chapter 2 Reason to Fear

1. Harris, *End of Faith*, 44.

2. Ibid., 29–33.

3. Ibid., 84.

4. John Adams, quoted in Dawkins, *God Delusion*, 43.

5. Joseph Brean, "A Day in the Intellectual Glare of Hitchens," *National Post* 18, November 2007, A1, A3.

6. Ibid.

7. Brian Bethune, "Is God Poison?" *Maclean's*, April 16, 2007, 42.

8. Harris, *End of Faith*, 45.

9. Ibid., 19.

10. Ibid., 23.

11. Ibid., 17.

12. Quoted in Dawkins, *God Delusion*, 306.

13. Harris, *End of Faith*, 17.

14. Dawkins, *God Delusion*, 304.

15. Nehru, quoted in ibid., 45.

16. Dawkins, *God Delusion*, 33.

17. Adler, "New Naysayers," 48.

18. Alister McGrath and Joanna Collicutt McGrath, *The Dawkins Delusion* (Downers Grove, IL: InterVarsity, 2007), 25.

19. Richard Swinburne, quoted in Dawkins, *God Delusion*, 65.

20. Dawkins, *God Delusion*, 51–54.

21. Ibid., 319.

22. Harris, *End of Faith*, 76.

23. Ibid., 13, 17, 31, 65.

24. Dawkins, *God Delusion*, 99.

25. Ibid., 237–39. However, without in any way minimizing the terrible representation of God and Christianity, I must note that Dawkins was quoting a cyber legend; Robertson actually referred to abortion as the cause of the damage in New Orleans, although he has made controversial comments about homosexuality at other times (see http://www.snopes.com/katrina/satire/robertson.asp).

26. Ibid., 245.

27. Ibid., 242–43.

28. See Adler, "New Naysayers," 48–49.

29. Dawkins, *God Delusion*, 31.

30. Ibid., 263.

31. Quotations and other information from Tamarin's study are taken from ibid., 255–57.

32. Ibid., 250.

33. Harris, *End of Faith*, 36–38.

34. Ibid., 31.

35. Ibid., 38.

36. Bethune, "Is God Poison?" 44.

37. Harris, *End of Faith*, 128–29.

38. Alan Bloom, *The Closing of the American Mind* (New York: Simon and Schuster, 1987), 25–26.

39. For a brief analysis of the cultural causes of the lofty status assigned to tolerance, see Bloom, *Closing of the American Mind*, 25–26.

40. Harris, *End of Faith*, 13.

41. Dawkins, *God Delusion*, 286.

42. Ibid., 289–90.

43. Ibid., 291.

44. Gary Potter, quoted in Dawkins, *God Delusion*, 290.

45. Randall Terry, quoted in ibid., 292.

46. Sam Harris, *Letter to a Christian Nation*, quoted in Dawkins, *God Delusion*, 342.

47. See also Adler, "New Naysayers," 49.

Chapter 3 Religion and Violence

1. McGrath and McGrath, *Dawkins Delusion*, 22.

2. Gary Potter, quoted in Dawkins, *God Delusion*, 290. Dawkins states he has taken this and the subsequent quotes from the website http://adultthought.ucsd.edu/ Culture_War/The_American_Taliban.html.

3. Randall Terry, quoted in Dawkins, *God Delusion*, 290.

4. Fred Phelps, quoted in ibid., 290–91.

5. McGrath and McGrath, *Dawkins Delusion*, 14, 22.

6. Ibid., 13.

7. This true story is taken from dc Talk and Voice of the Martyrs, *Jesus Freaks: Stories of Those Who Stood for Jesus, the Ultimate Jesus Freaks* (Tulsa, OK: Albury Publishing, 1999), 30–35. For many similar stories, see the Voice of the Martyrs website, http://www.persecution.com.

8. Paul Marshall, ed., *Religious Freedom in the World: A Global Report on Freedom and Persecution* (Nashville: Broadman and Holman, 2000).

9. Paul Marshall, *Their Blood Cries Out: The Worldwide Tragedy of Modern Christians Who Are Dying for Their Faith* (Nashville: Thomas Nelson, 1997), 122.

10. Anna Dickinson, "Quantifying Religious Oppression: Russian Orthodox Church Closures and Repression of Priests 1917–1941," *Religion, State and Society* 28 (2000): 327–35, quoted in McGrath and McGrath, *Dawkins Delusion*, 78.

11. Marshall, *Religious Freedom*, 99–101.

12. Marshall, *Their Blood Cries Out*, 75–79.

13. Ibid., 78.

14. Marshall, *Religious Freedom*, 101–3.

15. Dawkins, *God Delusion*, 273, 278.

16. See Robert A. Pape, *Dying to Win: The Strategic Logic of Suicide Terrorism* (New York: Random House, 2005) for a fuller explanation of the political motivations behind suicide attacks. See also Diego Gambetta, ed., *Making Sense of Suicide Missions* (Oxford: Oxford University Press), 2005.

17. Robert Louis Wilken, "Roots of Jihad," *First Things*, October 2003, 67–68.

18. Charles Taylor, *Reconciling the Solitudes: Essays on Canadian Federalism and Nationalism*, ed. Guy Laforest (Montreal: McGill-Queen's University Press, 2005), 45.

19. Kevin Michael Grace, "Just a Few 'Young Toughs,'" *Alberta Report Newsmagazine* 28, no. 3, February 5, 2001, 15.

20. Ingrid Peritz, "Include 'Values of Quebec Nation' in Provincial Charter, PQ Says," *The Globe and Mail* 15, December 2007, A16.

21. Steve Chase, "No Thanks for the Memories," *Alberta Report Newsmagazine* 21, no. 9, February 14, 1994.

22. Barry Came, "Lasagna Unmasked," *MacClean's* 106, no. 13, March 29, 1993.

23. Bernard Lewis, *The Crisis of Islam: Holy War and Unholy Terror* (New York: Modern Library, 2003), 63.

24. John C. Zimmerman, "Roots of Conflict: The Islamist Critique of Western Value," *Journal of Social, Political, and Economic Studies* 30, no. 4, Winter 2005, 426.

25. Hasan al-Banna, *Selected Writings of Hasan al-Banna Shaheed* (Karachi: International Islamic Publishers, 1983), 63, 153–56.

26. Sayyid Qutb, *This Religion of Islam* (Palo Alto: Al Manar Press, 1967), 25.

27. Zimmerman, "Roots of Conflict," 435–39.

28. Ibid., 433. For a fuller understanding of the views of Ayatollah Khomeini, also see Amir Taheri, *Holy Terror: The Inside Story of Islamic Terrorism* (London: Sphere Books, 1987).

29. For more information on this phenomenon, see Malise Ruthven, *Fundamentalism: The Search for Meaning* (Oxford: Oxford University Press, 2004).

30. McGrath and McGrath, *Dawkins Delusion*, 81.

31. Gwynne Dyer, *War* (Toronto: Random House, 2005), 230–31.

32. Guglielmo Ferrero, *Peace and War* (London: Macmillan, 1933), 63–64.

33. Dyer, *War*, 231, 236.

34. To understand how important binary oppositions can be in wider discourse, social divisions, and human interaction, see Kathy Mills, "Deconstructing Binary Oppositions in Literacy Discourse and Pedagogy," *Australian Journal of Language and Literacy* 28 (2005): 67–82.

35. For a discussion of the long-running Catholic-Protestant division, see Michael Wheeler, *The Old Enemies: Catholic and Protestant in Nineteenth-Century English Culture* (Cambridge: Cambridge University Press, 2006). For a further analysis of how identities are formed in a world full of flux, see Stephen E. Cornell and Douglas Hartmann, *Ethnicity and Race: Making Identities in a Changing World* (Thousand Oaks, CA: Pine Forge, 1998).

36. Darryl Li, "Echoes of Violence," in *The New Killing Fields: Massacre and the Politics of Intervention*, ed. Nicolaus Mills and Kira Brunner (New York: Basic Books, 2003), 121.

Chapter 4 Is Christianity Irrational and Devoid of Evidence?

1. Harris, *End of Faith*, 17.

2. Ibid., 19.

3. For a fuller discussion of the issues of rationality, justification, warrant, evidence, and other related matters, see Alvin Plantinga, *Warranted Christian Belief* (New York: Oxford University Press, 2000), 67–70.

4. C. S. Lewis, *Surprised by Joy: The Shape of My Early Life* (New York: Harcourt Brace, 1955), 221.

5. For two good examples of Paul's use of evidence for different kinds of audiences, see Acts 13, where he gives evidence to a Jewish audience of Jesus's messiahship, and Acts 17, where he addresses an educated Gentile audience and appeals to their own philosophers to make his case for Jesus's resurrection and future judgment over the earth.

6. Wolfhart Pannenberg, *"Ist Jesus wirklich auferstanden?"* in *Ist Jesus wirklich auferstanden? Geistliche Woche fur Sudwestdeutschland der Evang. Akademie Mannheim vom 16. bis 23. Februar 1964* (Karlsruhe: Evangelische Akademie Mannheim, 1964), 24.

7. Rudolph Bultmann, *Faith and Understanding I*, 6th ed., R. W. Funk, trans. L. P. Smith (London: SCM, 1969), 83.

8. For a healthy discussion of the evidence for and against the resurrection of Jesus, see Gary Habermas and Antony Flew, *Did Jesus Rise from the Dead?* ed. Terry L. Miethe (San Francisco: Harper and Row, 1987). Other helpful books setting out evidence for Jesus's resurrection and a number of other important Christian truth claims are N. T. Wright, *The Challenge of Jesus: Rediscovering Who Jesus Was and Is* (Downers Grove, IL: InterVarsity, 1999), and William Lane Craig, *Reasonable Faith: Christian Truth and Apologetics*, 3rd ed. (Wheaton: Crossway, 1994).

9. Harris, *End of Faith*, 64–65.

10. Canadian theologian D. H. Lunn is currently writing a work that will attempt to demonstrate that evangelical theology contains an explanation for the coherence of faith in a wholly good and all-powerful God despite the existence of natural evil.

11. Alvin Plantinga, *God, Freedom, and Evil* (Grand Rapids: Eerdmans, 1974), 10.

12. McGrath and McGrath, *Dawkins Delusion*, 25.

13. Ibid., 24–26.

14. Dawkins, *God Delusion*, 51–54.

15. Alvin Plantinga, "Two Dozen (or So) Theistic Arguments," lecture at Calvin College, http://www.calvin.edu/academic/philosophy/virtual_library/articles/plantinga_alvin/two_dozen_or_so_theistic_arguments.pdf (accessed February 16, 2009).

16. Kai Nielsen, *Reason and Practice: A Modern Introduction to Philosophy* (New York: Harper and Row, 1971), 143–44, italics mine.

17. Dawkins, *God Delusion*, 33.

18. Millard Erickson, *Christian Theology* (Grand Rapids: Baker Books, 1998), 346.

19. Ibid., 346–67.

20. C. S. Lewis, *Mere Christianity* (San Francisco: HarperCollins, 1980), 161–62.

21. Richard Swinburne, quoted in Dawkins, *God Delusion*, 65.

22. Dawkins, *God Delusion*, 50.

23. Ibid., 65.

24. Harris, *End of Faith*, 96.

25. Blaise Pascal, *Pensees*, trans. A. J. Krailsheimer (Baltimore: Penguin Books, 1966), 149.

26. Thomas Nagel, *The Last Word* (New York: Oxford University Press, 1997), 130, italics mine.

27. Pascal, *Pensees*, sec. 234, italics mine.

28. Swinburne, quoted in Dawkins, *God Delusion*, 65.

29. Dawkins, *God Delusion*, 77–79.

Chapter 5 Is Christianity Anti-Scientific?

1. Dawkins, *God Delusion*, 319.

2. Harris, *End of Faith*, 76.

3. Ibid., 13, 17, 31, 65.

4. James W. Sire, *Naming the Elephant: Worldview as a Concept* (Downers Grove: InterVarsity, 2004), 19.

5. Gilbert K. Chesterton, *Heretics/Orthodoxy* (Nashville: Thomas Nelson, 2000), 279–80.

6. Dawkins, *God Delusion*, 284–85.

7. Stephen Jay Gould, "Impeaching a Self-Appointed Judge," *Scientific American* 267, no. 1, 1992. See also Gould's book, *Rock of Ages: Science and Religion in the Fullness of Life* (New York: Ballantine, 2002), for a wider discussion of the relationship of science and religion.

8. Dawkins, *God Delusion*, 57.

9. Rodney Stark, *For the Glory of God: How Monotheism Led to Reformations, Science, Witch-hunts, and the End of Slavery* (Princeton: Princeton University Press, 2003), 124.

10. St. Augustine, *The Literal Meaning of Genesis*, translated and annotated by John Hammond Taylor, S.J., 2 vols. (New York: Newman Press, 1982), 1:41.

11. For a fuller discussion of Augustine's views on the interpretation of biblical texts relating to the origin of the world, see Davis A. Young, "The Contemporary Relevance of Augustine's View of Creation," *Perspectives on Science and Christian Faith* 40, no. 1 (1988): 42–45.

12. Augustine, *Literal Meaning of Genesis*, 42–43.

13. Nancy R. Pearcey and Charles B. Thaxton, *The Soul of Science: Christian Faith and Natural Philosophy* (Wheaton: Crossway Books, 1994), 19.

14. Stark, *For the Glory of God*, 124.

15. Ibid., 147.

16. Melvin Calvin, *Chemical Evolution* (Oxford: Clarendon Press, 1969), 258.

17. Alfred North Whitehead, quoted in Stark, *For the Glory of God*, 147.

18. Ibid., 148.

19. Pearcey and Thaxton, *Soul of Science*, 23–24.

20. Stark, *For the Glory of God*, 149.

21. For further reading on the question of the presence or absence of science in non-Christian civilizations, see Pearcey and Thaxton, *Soul of Science*, and Stark, *For the Glory of God*, 124.

22. Bertrand Russell, *The Problem of China* (London: George Allen and Unwin, 1922), 193.

23. Joseph Needham, *Science and Civilization in China*, 6 vols. (Cambridge: Cambridge University Press, 1954–1984), l:581.

Chapter 6 Is Biblical Morality Appalling?

1. Dawkins, *God Delusion*, 31.

2. McGrath and McGrath, *Dawkins Delusion*, 89.

3. Dawkins, *God Delusion*, 253.

4. Ibid., 241.

5. Ibid., 243.

6. C. S. Lewis, *The Problem of Pain* (Glasgow: Fountain Books, 1940), 21–22.

7. Dawkins, *God Delusion*, 251.

8. Ibid., 257.

9. Two such warning passages are Isaiah 10 and 47, in which God spells out judgment on people for their wickedness and rejection of him.

10. See also Lamentations 3:33, where the author of that book laments about the grief God experiences when he finds it necessary to send judgment upon a people.

11. Plantinga, *God, Freedom, and Evil*, 10.

Chapter 7 Living the Way Jesus Calls Us to Live

1. John Redekop, "The Biblical Roots of Liberal Democracy," unpublished paper, Canadian Christian Political Science Association, June 3, 2008, 2.

2. Lewis, *Mere Christianity*, 78.

3. Analects of Confucius, 15:39, italics mine.

4. C. S. Lewis, *The Abolition of Man* (New York: Harper, 2001), 45–46.

5. Douglas Todd, "Christian Soldiers March to a New Tune," *Vancouver Sun* 23, December 2006, C5.

6. Redekop, *"The Biblical Roots of Liberal Democracy,"* 12.

7. Thomas Hobbes, *Leviathan: Parts One and Two* (Indianapolis: Bobbs-Merrill, 1958), 107.

8. David Moberg made this statement as part of his endorsement of Alvin J. Schmidt's book *How Christianity Changed the World* (Grand Rapids: Zondervan, 2004).

Chapter 8 Christianity's Gifts to the World

1. Frederick Farrar, *The Early Days of Christianity* (New York: A. L. Burt, 1882), 71.

2. Polybius, *Histories*, 6.

3. James S. Denis, *Social Evils of the Non-Christian World* (New York: Revell, 1898), 69–70.

4. *Didache*, in *The Apostolic Fathers*, trans. Kirsopp Lake (Cambridge: Harvard University Press, 1955), l:319.

5. Michael W. Holmes, ed., *Apostolic Fathers in English*, 3rd ed. (Grand Rapids: Baker Academic, 2006), 196.

6. Schmidt, *How Christianity Changed the World*, 52.

7. Ibid.

8. Clement of Alexandria, *The Instructor*, in *The Ante-Nicene Fathers*, ed. Alexander Roberts and James Donaldson (Grand Rapids: Eerdmans, 1982–83), 2:279.

9. Tertullian, *Apology*, in *The Ante-Nicene Fathers*, 3:24–25.

10. Schmidt, *How Christianity Changed the World*, 52.

11. Ibid., 133.

12. Ibid.

13. Justin Martyr, *Apology*, 67.

14. Tertullian, *Apology*, 39.

15. Edward Ryan, *The History of the Effects of Religion on Mankind: In Countries Ancient and Modern, Barbarous and Civilized* (Dublin: T. M. Bates, 1802), 132. For background information on the *Apostolic Constitutions*, see also Bruno Steimer, "Apostolic Constitutions," in *Dictionary of Early Christian Literature*, ed. Siegmar Döpp and Wilhem Geerlings, trans. Matthew O'Connell (New York: Crossroad, 2000), 44; and E. A. Livingstone and F. L. Cross, eds., "Apostolic Constitutions," in *The Oxford Dictionary of the Christian Church*, 3rd ed. (Oxford: Oxford University Press, 1997), 90.

16. J. Beaudry, "Orphans in the Early Church," in *New Catholic Encyclopedia* (New York: McGraw-Hill, 1967), 10:785.

17. C. Schmidt, *The Social Results of Early Christianity*, trans. R. W. Dale (London: Wm. Isbister, 1889), 327.

18. Cyril J. Davey, "George Müller," in *Great Leaders of the Christian Church*, ed. John Woodbridge (Chicago: Moody, 1988), 320.

19. Matthew A. Crenson, *Building the Invisible Orphanage: A History of the American Welfare System* (Cambridge: Harvard University Press, 1998), 26.

20. Schmidt, *How Christianity Changed the World*, 134. Scripture quotations are from the New International Version.

21. Roger J. Green, *The Life and Ministry of William Booth: Founder of the Salvation Army* (Nashville: Abingdon Press, 2005), 109, 111, 114, 130.

22. Ibid., 166–68. For a further treatment of the history and work of the Salvation Army, see David Malcolm Bennett, *The General: William Booth* (Longwood, FL: Xulon Press, 2003).

23. L. L. Doggett, *History of the Young Men's Christian Association* (New York: International Committee of Young Men's Christian Association, 1896), 47, 116.

24. Owen E. Pense, "Young Men's Christian Association," in *The World Book Encyclopedia* (Chicago: Field Enterprises Educational Corporation, 1958), 18:8978.

25. Schmidt, *How Christianity Changed the World*, 141–42.

26. Cited in Martin Gumpert, *Dunant: The Story of the Red Cross* (New York: Oxford University Press, 1938), 300.

27. Ibid., 63. See also D. James Kennedy and Jerry Newcombe, *What if Jesus Had Never Been Born?* (Nashville: Thomas Nelson, 1994), 152.

28. Schmidt, *How Christianity Changed the World*, 152.

29. Dionysius, *Works of Dionysius*, epistle 12:5.

30. Ibid., 12:4.

31. Howard W. Haggard, *The Doctor in History* (New York: Yale University Press, 1934), 108.

32. Rodney Stark, *The Rise of Early Christianity: A Sociologist Considers History* (Princeton: Princeton University Press, 1996), 86.

33. Haggard, *Doctor in History*, 78.

34. George E. Gask and John Todd, "The Origin of Hospitals" in *Science, Medicine, and History*, ed. E. Ashworth Underwood (New York: Arno Press, 1975), 122.

35. Gerhard Uhlhorn, *Christian Charity in the Ancient Church* (New York: Charles Schribner's Sons, 1883), 323.

36. David Riesman, *The Story of Medicine in the Middle Ages* (New York: Harper and Brothers, 1936), 355.

37. Ralph Jackson, *Doctors and Diseases in the Roman Empire* (Norman, OK: University of Oklahoma Press, 1988).

38. For a broad discussion of the origin of hospitals and early Christianity's role in it, see Schmidt, *How Christianity Changed the World*, 152–60.

39. Nathaniel W. Faxon, *The Hospital in Contemporary Life* (Cambridge: Harvard University Press, 1949), 7.

40. Riesman, *Story of Medicine*, 356.

41. C. F. V. Smout, *The Story of the Progress of Medicine* (Bristol, UK: John Wright and Sons, 1964), 40.

42. Faxon, *Hospital in Contemporary Life*, 10.

43. E. Nasalli-Rocca, "Hospitals, History of," in *New Catholic Encyclopedia* (New York: McGraw-Hill, 1967), 3:160.

44. David R. James, "Slavery and Involuntary Servitude," in *Encyclopedia of Sociology*, ed. Edgar F. Borgatta and Marie L. Borgatta (New York: Macmillan, 1992), 4:1792.

45. Schmidt, *How Christianity Changed the World*, 272.

46. Aristotle, *Politics* 1.1255, *Nichomachean Ethics*, 8.11.

47. Brian Eads, "Slavery's Shameful Return to Africa," *Reader's Digest*, March 1996, 77–81.

48. Schmidt, *How Christianity Changed the World*, 276.

49. Cited in ibid., 274.

50. Augustine, *The City of God*, 19:15.

51. W. E. H. Lecky, *History of European Morals: From Augustus to Charlemagne*, vol. 2 (New York: D. Appleton, 1926), 76–78. For a fuller discussion of Christianity's influence in the emancipation and progress of slaves, see also Schmidt, *How Christianity Changed the World*, 272–91.

52. Robin Lane Fox, *Pagans and Christians* (San Francisco: Perennial Library, 1986), 298.

53. Lecky, *History of European Morals*, vol. 1, 69.

54. Ryan, *History of the Effects of Religion*, 151.

55. Lecky, *History of European Morals*, vol. 2, 71.

56. Kenneth Scott Latourette, *A History of Christianity* (New York: Harper and Brothers, 1953), 558.

57. Garth Lean, *God's Politician* (Colorado Springs: Helmers and Howard, 1987), 47. For a more exhaustive biography of William Wilberforce, see John Pollock's well-known book, *Wilberforce* (Belleville, MI: Lion, 1986).

58. Kennedy and Newcombe, *What if Jesus Had Never Been Born?* 21.

59. For a fuller description of William Wilberforce's life and fight against slavery, see John Stoughton, *William Wilberforce* (New York: A. C. Armstrong and Son, 1880); and Pollock's book, *Wilberforce* (Belleville, MI: Lion, 1986).

60. For an explanation and analysis of the strategies employed by Wilberforce in his battles against slavery, child labor, harsh debtor laws, and other social evils, see Chamberlain, *Talking about Good and Bad without Getting Ugly: A Guide to Moral Persuasion* (Downers Grove, IL: InterVarsity, 2005), 103–26.

61. Schmidt, *How Christianity Changed the World*, 171.

62. Ibid., 186–87.

63. Stark, *For the Glory of God*, 63. Stark mentions in a footnote in his book that recently some historians have come to believe there were universities in Ireland as early as the sixth century, the most famous one being at Clonmacnois. This claim has credibility since Irish scholars were widely admired at that time and were welcomed in the catechetical schools of Europe. These institutions, if they existed, seem to have been destroyed during the Norse occupation.

64. Stark, *For the Glory of God*, 62–63.

65. George H. Marsden, *The Outrageous Idea of Christian Scholarship* (New York: Oxford University Press, 1997), 15.

66. Stark, *For the Glory of God*, 63.

67. Donald Tewksbury, *The Founding of American Colleges and Universities before the Civil War* (New York: Teachers College Columbia University, 1932), 82.

68. Schmidt, *How Christianity Changed the World*, 190.

69. Matthew Parris, "As an atheist, I truly believe Africa needs God: Missionaries, not aid money, are the solution to Africa's biggest problem—the crushing passivity of the people's mindset," *Times Online*, December 27, 2008, http://www.timesonline.co.uk/tol/comment/columnists/matthew_parris/article5400568.ece (accessed January 20, 2009).

Chapter 9 Is There a Way Forward?

1. McGrath and McGrath, *Dawkins Delusion*, 81.

2. G. K. Chesterton, quoted in Philip Yancey, *Soul Survivor: How My Faith Survived the Church* (New York: Doubleday, 2001), 58.

3. For further data and argumentation on the dating and historical reliability of the Gospels, see F. F. Bruce, *The New Testament Documents: Are They Reliable?* 5th ed. (Downers Grove, IL: InterVarsity, 1970), especially 13–19; and Craig, *Reasonable Faith*, especially 334–37.

4. Lewis, *Mere Christianity*, 55.

5. Ibid., 127.

Index

167

Paul Chamberlain (PhD, Marquette University) is director of the Institute of Christian Apologetics and professor of apologetics, ethics, and philosophy of religion at Trinity Western University in Langley, British Columbia. He has also served on the staff of Ravi Zacharias International Ministries. He is the author of *Can We Be Good without God?* and *Final Wishes*.